The Big Shift

THE BIG SHIFT

The Seismic Change in Canadian Politics, Business, and Culture and What It Means for Our Future

DARRELL BRICKER & JOHN IBBITSON

HarperCollins*Publishers*Ltd

HarperCollins Publishers Ltd
2 Bloor Street East, 20th Floor
Toronto, Ontario, Canada
M4W 1A8

www.harpercollins.ca

Library and Archives Canada Cataloguing in Publication
information is available upon request

ISBN 978-1-44341-645-0

Printed and bound in the United States

RRD 9 8 7 6 5 4 3 2 1

To the loves of my life, Nina and Emily

D.B.

To the memory of my father

J.I.

Contents

The Big Shift

Preface

YOU NEED TO STOP LISTENING

In university classrooms across Canada, professors are teaching their students nonsense. In newspaper columns and on television, commentators are talking rot. Authors and playwrights and poets and musicians sing of a country that doesn't exist. Politicians offer promises that people don't want them to keep.

You need to stop listening to these people. Not because they're left-wing or right-wing, but because they're just wrong.

The people we're talking about are mostly found in the classrooms and boardrooms and newsrooms in the big cities of Ontario and Quebec. We call them the Laurentian elites. They are a small, select group, found in Central Canada's major centres, who up until very recently controlled the political and cultural levers of the country. Although they often disagree among themselves, they share a common set of assumptions about Canada: that it's a fragile nation; that the federal government's job is to bind together a country that would otherwise fall apart; that the biggest challenge is keeping Quebec inside Confederation; that the poorer regions must forever stay poor, propped up by the richer parts of the country; that the national identity—whatever it is—must be protected from the American juggernaut; that Canada is a helpful fixer in the world, a peacekeeper, a joiner of all the best clubs.

Most of all, these Laurentian elites assume that their version of the country *is* the country, and that they run the country, just as they have always run it in the past.

All of this and more, put together, we call the Laurentian Consensus. We think the Consensus is an illusion. We think the country has irrevocably changed from a place it controlled and understood to one it no longer controls or understands. This change, the most fundamental Canada has experienced since the social revolutions of the 1960s, we call the Big Shift.

For about 20 years, Canada has been importing roughly a quarter of a million people a year from other countries. That's a new Toronto every 10 years. If you reproduce the country's largest city twice in such a short period of time, you're going to change things. If those two new Torontos consist almost entirely of immigrants from third world countries, mixing with a population of largely European stock, you're going to change things a lot. If you keep doing it—year after year—the country will soon become unrecognizable.

The Laurentian elites don't realize that Canada no longer belongs to them. A country that was once white is becoming brown. A country that was once part of the Atlantic world is becoming part of the Pacific world. The provinces that mattered most don't matter as much anymore. The country's centre has shifted west, and power has shifted with it. In fact, power is now shared by two groups: Westerners and Ontario's suburban middle class, especially the immigrant suburban middle class. In terms of power and priorities, nothing else and no one else is as important.

The Laurentian elites don't get this. Ensconced in their leafy downtown enclaves—Toronto's Annex, Ottawa's Glebe, Montreal's Outremont—shuddering at the faceless suburbs they pass through on the way to the cottage, they think their values are still the nation's values and their assumptions the nation's assumptions. Because they stand at the front of so many classrooms, and still run or work for the biggest newspapers, networks, and publishing houses, because they sit around so many boardrooms—because, in short, they remain the gatekeepers to Central Canada's academic, business, and cultural communities—and because they talk only to each other and to no one else, they continue to think they matter.

They don't matter. The country has moved beyond their understanding. This leaves the Laurentian elites angry and bewildered. Nothing makes sense the way it used to. They're like the Catholic Church during the Renaissance, trying to keep the Earth at the centre of the universe despite everything the astronomers were telling them. So they contort reality to make it fit their false assumptions, even as their contortions become increasingly ridiculous.

You may think that this is a conservative argument. It isn't. Yes, the Conservatives under Stephen Harper understand better than anyone else what Canada is becoming. They have tailored their message and their priorities to fit the New Canada. They get the Big Shift.

But the values and priorities of the New Canada aren't entirely—or even mostly—conservative. They're realistic, pragmatic, cosmopolitan, global, forward thinking. Progressive politicians should be able to speak to them, too. Thomas Mulcair and his rapidly evolving New Democratic Party are trying to do just that. The Liberal Party, which was always the party that most closely identified with the Laurentian Consensus, still doesn't seem to get any of this. And so it's dying. It is not, however, dead yet. Whether the party of Laurier and King and Trudeau and Chrétien—but also of Turner and Martin and Dion and Ignatieff—recovers and thrives depends entirely on whether it wakes up to what has happened to a country that it no longer comprehends.

Some readers may consider what we're about to say to be treason—not against our country (though some may think that, too) but against our class. For we are the people we are warning you about. Darrell Bricker is the president of Ipsos Reid Public Affairs, a major pollster in Canada and around the world. John Ibbitson is the chief political writer for the *Globe and Mail.* We're a couple of middle-aged WASPs who live in Laurentian neighbourhoods, who work for companies that are information leaders, who for much of our careers have shared and traded on the very assumptions we now reject.

But that's why we've written this book. We realize that the Canada we thought we knew has gone away. Everything has changed, and everyone must change with it or step aside.

Otherwise you won't listen to us anymore.

1

The Death of the Laurentian Consensus
WHY THE PEOPLE WHO USED
TO MATTER MOST DON'T ANYMORE

The first course was asparagus soup. Not too much cream, because everyone eats sensibly nowadays. But asparagus is in season for such a short time, and it was such a decadent contrast to the lamb and couscous. Things were going so well until Gerald brought up politics, as Gerald always must.

"Do you see what he's done now?"

"Who?" Celia asked.

"Who do you think?" Gerald growled, mopping the bowl with his bread. "He's cutting funding to the National Ballet."

"No!" Celia lowered her spoon.

Gerald nodded grimly. "*And* the Canadian Opera Company. *And* the Toronto Symphony."

They were silent for a moment. The spring rain washed softly across the leaded glass panes of the dining room window.

"Are you sure?" Roberta tried to hide her alarm, for

Gerald could easily ruin an entire evening if he got going. "I thought that was just what the Opposition was claiming."

"Oh, he's going to do it, all right, just you wait." Gerald leaned back, clenching the napkin in his right hand. "He *hates* the arts. Can't stand 'em."

"Such a damn shame," Maurice muttered, holding up his bowl. "Roberta, are there seconds?"

"I could live with the tax cuts." The guests exchanged quiet glances. Gerald was off and running again. "I could live with the tax cuts, though they're all wrong." His scowl deepened. "I could live with the nonsense about Israel, even if it does destroy 50 years of Canadian diplomacy." He tossed the napkin on the table in disgust. "But Kyoto. Simply walking away from Kyoto. Walking away!"

People clucked sympathetically. Gerald could be tiresome, but he was right.

"And the prisons, when crime is going down. Putting boys in jail with hardened criminals for keeping a couple of plants—"

"Well, six, actually," Roberta corrected, but nobody was listening.

"I smoked pot when I was in college. Everybody did." Gerald stuck out his chin as though daring contradiction. But most of his table companions still smoked when the kids were away on the weekend.

"It's this law-and-order garbage, and this ramming everything through without thinking—and gutting the census—*gutting it!*—and this kowtowing to the Americans, and if it's not the Americans it's the Chinese—"

"The Internet snooping bill's what frightens me," Maurice interjected, hoping to guide the conversation to calmer waters. "I was talking the other day to one of the guys in IT. And he said—"

But no luck. Gerald was under full sail.

"*And* the Internet snooping bill. *And* beating the bureaucracy into submission. *And* that spectacle at the G20. *And* shutting down that water research station. And *especially* what they did to Irwin Cotler." The Tories—who, everyone knew, coveted Cotler's Montreal riding—had been circulating rumours that the Liberal MP was stepping down, which Cotler adamantly denied.

"Poor Irwin." Celia shook her head sadly.

"They're all just a bunch of thugs." Gerald was out of his chair, leaning over the table. "A bunch of thugs. Stole the election, that's what they did! You saw what happened in Guelph." Robocalls directing Liberal supporters to non-existent polling stations. Shocking.

"And it wasn't just Guelph, if you ask me." Maurice lowered his voice, as if they were being overheard. "I think it was *everywhere.*"

"He's the worst prime minister we've ever had. Why can't people see that?" Gerald, his face flushed, pounded the table with his fist. "Why can't those damned Brampton Sikhs *see* that?"

Maurice was out of his chair, his arm around Gerald's shoulder. "Come on, my friend, let's get some air."

"Damned thugs." Gerald's voice trailed through the air as Maurice guided him to the front porch. "That's all they are. Just a bunch of damned thugs."

––––––––

You might have witnessed a conversation such as this. It could have been at a dinner party in any comfortable neighbourhood in any Central Canadian city that has a decent university in it. Or maybe you were at a restaurant, or a reception. Maybe it was over a Guinness in a pub, or on a squash court. Maybe you were just listening in. Or maybe you're one of them yourself.

They are the Laurentian Consensus. From the time of Confederation until quite recently, the political, academic, cultural, media, and business elites in the communities along the watershed of the St. Lawrence River ran this country. On all of the great issues of the day, these Laurentian elites debated among themselves, reached a consensus, and implemented that consensus. They governed.

These elites are in a very bad mood right now—the worst in their lives, as far as politics is concerned. No one is listening to them anymore. At one level they understand this; at another they don't. It's impossible for them to comprehend the influence they have lost. The Laurentian Consensus in eclipse? Nonsense. You might as well claim the CBC is irrelevant.

What happened to the Laurentian Consensus, and why? What replaced it? What comes next? That is what this book is about.

———

How close should Canada's relationship with Great Britain be? How close should Canada be to the United States? What should we do about conscription? What should we do about the Depression? What should we do about poverty? What does Quebec want, and should we give it? How do we bring home the Constitution? What should we do about the deficit?

The Laurentian elites grappled with these and other great issues from the time of Confederation until not very long ago. The debates played out in the pages of the major newspapers, in books, on television, and on university campuses. But most of the discussion was held behind closed doors: in faculty clubs, the hallways of legislatures, in dining rooms. Especially in dining rooms.

The leading figures of the Consensus form the spine of Canadian political and cultural thought: George Brown, John A. Macdonald, George-Étienne Cartier, Ernest Lapointe, O.D. Skelton, Henri Bourassa, Harold Innis, Hume Wrong, Lester Pearson, Vincent Massey, George Grant, Walter Gordon, Marshall McLuhan, Bora Laskin, Pierre Trudeau, René Lévesque, Tom Kent, Charles Taylor, Lucien Bouchard, Jeffrey Simpson, Margaret Atwood,

Adrienne Clarkson, André Pratte. And these are just the names you might come up with off the top of your head.

Sometimes they couldn't agree and the voters had to decide, as they did in the free trade election of 1988. More often than not, however, the Laurentian elites forged a consensus by accommodating one another's concerns, and then presented that consensus to the public as a *fait accompli,* sometimes in the form of proposed legislation, sometimes through federal–provincial agreements, other times through simple social osmosis. The discussions over sherry or Scotch, the academic paper or editorial that made the rounds, the *quid* that both sides accepted in exchange for the *quo,* became that most entrenched of all wisdoms: conventional.

We need high tariffs to protect Canadian manufacturers from American competition. Conscription, yes, but as little of it as possible. Ottawa must take the lead in social policy, because only Ottawa has sufficient power to tax. Quebec can and must be accommodated, but within limits. The deficit is not the most important concern. The deficit *is* the most important concern.

Issue after issue, decade after decade, the Laurentian Consensus shaped the public policy arc of this country.

Its members were and are few enough that most of them knew or know each other. At first they were largely of British stock and largely Protestant, though any bias against the French, Catholics, or Jews was far from proscriptive; indeed, agreement between the French and English elites was essential, and whenever it was not obtained, things went badly. They were, for the most part, from the upper ranks of the middle class, though the membrane was permeable. They were almost invariably small-*l* liberals who voted for the large-*L* party. Indeed, the Liberal Party of Canada was the most obvious and powerful manifestation of the Laurentian Consensus.

But it would be wrong to say that the Laurentian Consensus and the Liberal Party were synonymous. Conservative governments, while treated with suspicion, were tolerated, provided they knew their place. R.B. Bennett created the forerunner of the Canadian Broadcasting Corporation, the official broadcaster of the Laurentian Consensus. Progressive Conservatives governed Ontario for 42 years. Brian Mulroney, who initially opposed free trade, embraced it when the Macdonald Commission's 1985 report signalled the consensus on tariffs had started to shift. Hugh Segal—once an aide to Ontario Premier Bill Davis, then an aspirant to the leadership of the Progressive Conservatives, and now a Conservative senator—still moves easily through the drawing rooms of the Laurentian elites, who didn't know how much they missed the Progressives Conservatives until they disappeared.

If a premier or prime minister did defy the Consensus, woe betide him. Why do we still today, more than 50 years later, see books, documentaries, and articles raging against John Diefenbaker's decision to cancel the Avro Arrow? Because he did so in defiance of the Laurentian Consensus, and the Consensus still hasn't forgiven him.

Yet we should not be stingy in our praise. If Canada is a great country—and we think it is—we have the Laurentian elites to thank. They guided us through two great and terrible wars, launched an infrastructure revolution in the 1950s that created the highways and airports we still use today. They pushed through the St. Lawrence Seaway, created a national social security system, nurtured cultural industries behind non-tariff walls, navigated the shoals of Quebec separatism (though it was a close-run thing), and brought home a Constitution with a Charter of Rights and Freedoms that is now emulated by more countries around the world than its American equivalent, and is watched over by a damn fine Supreme Court.

They did much, much else besides. The national parks system. Public broadcasting. The equalization program. The Canada Council.

Lord knows they had their flaws. Though they were no more anti-Semitic than was common at the time, it was enough to shut Canada's doors to Jews in the 1930s. How many died in concentration camps as a result? The internment of Japanese Canadians is a similar stain. The Consensus exhibited, and still exhibits, an anti-American chippiness that reflects its own famous insecurity. Canada was so much smaller than the United States, and so much more virtuous. It simply wasn't fair.

Worst of all—by far the worst of all—their treatment of Canada's Aboriginal peoples combined condescension, incomprehension, and a misdirected sense of guilt to produce policies that First Nations, Métis, and Inuit communities struggle to overcome to this day.[1]

But they got one big thing right: they created an open-door immigration policy that, starting in the 1960s, encouraged newcomers from Asia and elsewhere to immigrate to Canada. And that is why Canada is evolving so quickly into the word's first post-national state.

If the Laurentianists were honest, they'd admit this wasn't what they'd planned. For decades they had glumly pondered the failure of the Canadian nation. The French and English simply didn't get along that well; they never had, not since 1066. The French formed a nation within Canada, and Atlantic Canada jealously protected a discernible, though not definable, culture of its own. The rest of the country evolved into a collection of cities, farms, and bush that shared English as a common language and broadly embraced the Western ethos of capitalism, democracy, and the rule of law but otherwise had little in common despite Laurentian efforts to forge something, anything, that could be called a national culture.

The Canadian nation? There is no such thing, and never was.

But the inability of English and French to do more than tolerate each other produced a culture of accommodation that makes it possible for people of diverse backgrounds to live together in the largely urban, polyglot, intensely creative, and simply fabulous country that we celebrate today.

Open-door immigration combined with multicultural tolerance represents the finest achievement of the Laurentian elites. It has also helped do them in.

———

It was a beautiful July day, and the young boy was very excited because his grandmother was taking him to see a parade. The small town in central Ontario where they lived rarely hosted parades, and certainly there had never been a parade like this. The boy watched in awe as marching band followed float followed marching band. Men in bright sashes and their best Sunday suits walked proudly past, some carrying banners with phrases the boy didn't understand. A man with a grey beard dressed in a strange uniform cantered past on a high-spirited white horse. It was better than Christmas, but it was all very odd.

"What is the parade for?" John Ibbitson asked his grandmother, who still spoke with a Yorkshire lilt.

"To celebrate the Glorious Twelfth," she answered.

"What's the Glorious Twelfth?"

"It's the day we beat the Catholics."

Today the Orange Lodge is virtually extinct. But back in the 1960s its various local lodges could still come together to mount parades that filled the street for an hour. The settler culture that dominated central Ontario was fiercely anti-Catholic, except for those parts where Irish or Polish immigrants dominated, such as the Ottawa Valley. In places where the two cultures lived side by side, tensions often ran high on July 12, when Protestants celebrated the defeat of the Stuart armies at the Battle of the Boyne in 1690.

Protestant Canada voted Conservative, and because it voted Conservative, Liberals almost always won elections, thanks to Catholic immigrants. In the late 1800s, Canada had trouble attracting immigrants because most people coming to North America from Europe preferred to settle in the United States, where it was warmer and where there were already many of their own kind. Clifford Sifton, Wilfrid Laurier's minister of the interior, began aggressively recruiting new arrivals to fill the vast and mostly empty prairies. He launched what was effectively an immigration marketing campaign across Europe, promoting Canada as a welcoming host with plenty of good land and a much better-ordered society than its Wild West counterpart to the south. By the early 1900s, the country was increasingly the destination of Eastern Europeans, most of them Catholic or Jewish, who fled the pogroms and poverty of the old countries and whom the Americans perversely considered undesirables who would never fit in. Sifton famously described the ideal candidate as "a stalwart peasant in a sheepskin coat, born on the soil, whose forefathers have been peasants for 10 generations, with a stout wife and a half-dozen children."[2] The already established settlers in English Canada were suspicious of these waves of exotic immigrants, and the Conservative Party that they supported gained a reputation for being British, Protestant, and intolerant. Immigrants mostly shunned it, gratefully delivering their votes to the Liberal Party instead.

After the Second World War, millions abandoned a ravaged and impoverished Europe, filling Canada's cities with new arrivals from Italy and Portugal, from the Baltics and the Balkans. In 1967, the Liberal government of Lester Pearson lifted restrictions that for almost a century had sought to keep out Asian immigrants, especially the Chinese, either through a head tax or an outright ban. With each passing year, the country's largest cities became increasingly cosmopolitan, and the Laurentian Consensus embraced the spirit and policy of multiculturalism. This encouraged all ethnicities to live together, free to preserve their own culture while contributing to the stew of languages, customs, and cuisine that now dominates in Toronto, Vancouver, Montreal, and increasingly in the Prairie cities as well. Canadian multiculturalism self-consciously rejected the American melting pot alternative, where people were encouraged to submerge their native cultures and embrace the American ideal. Multiculturalism effectively (and guiltily) assumed that there was no Canadian ideal to aspire to; ironically, over the decades, multiculturalism itself became an ideal that was uniquely Canadian.

From the Irish Catholics to the Vietnamese, from the Poles to the Sikhs, new Canadians voted overwhelmingly for the Liberal Party, ensuring its dominance, while old, English, rural Canada watched resentfully and voted Tory in futile protest. When the Progressive Conservatives disintegrated in schism during the 1990s, the tendency by immigrants to vote Liberal was only reinforced. Data based on the 2008 Canada Election Survey revealed that in 2000 only 20 percent of immigrant voters were inclined toward either the Progressive Conservatives or the Canadian Alliance, while 70 percent supported the Liberals.

And then things started to shift. As if reaching a tipping point, the massive influx of new Canadians began rethinking its political allegiances. And in what seemed to be in defiance of all its best interests, the New Canada—the Canada of new Canadians, the urban, polyglot, multicultural mélange—swung its allegiance behind Old Canada, rural Canada, Prairie Canada, the Canada of the descendants of the Orange Lodge.

———

As a pollster, Darrell Bricker often speaks to national trade associations on the changing face of Canada. Often these meetings are held in Toronto and sometimes those organizations represent farmers. As he looks out on his audience, Bricker is struck by how people all look the same. Many of them are still a bit intimidated by the big city. And as Bricker rolls through the statistics that reveal just how profoundly the country is changing, he knows that he speaks to a room that defies those statistics. So he asks them: "Look around. How closely does this room reflect the changes I'm talking about?" He is always greeted with nervous laughter. They know the obvious.

Then Bricker gives them an assignment. They should take Toronto's subway from north to south, from east to west. They should look at the people on the subway. How many look like them? They should get off at a couple of stations and take a taste tour of Toronto. Can they smell the kimchi wafting through Koreatown, near Christie station? Or they should sample the dim sum you can find near St. Patrick station, or the naan bread in Little India, just south of Coxwell station.

If they prefer to drive, they should head to Brampton, look at the faces on the street, the signs in the windows. This is what people mean when they talk about the large influx of South Asians to Canada. Or do the same in Richmond Hill, with its large Sino-Canadian population.

Then Bricker asks his bemused farmers one final question: "What are you growing and raising for these people?" Many of them consider it an innovation to offer free-range eggs and organic lettuce to locavores in farmers' markets. But what they really need to understand, Bricker tells them, is how milk products are used in Chinese and South Asian cuisines. These people are the new consumers, and they are the only ones having kids.

But it's not just farmers who don't understand Canada's newest generation. The Laurentian Consensus doesn't understand them either, even though they were the ones who made their ascendancy possible.

Since 2006, Canada has had more population growth than any country in the G8. Our population is up 5.9 percent from what it was five years ago, according to Statistics Canada. About a third of this increase is due to natural population growth (more people being born than dying). The other two-thirds—67 percent, to be precise—is due to immigration. By comparison, in the same period, the population of the United States increased by 4.4 percent, with most of the increase coming from natural population growth. At this rate, our population will catch up with theirs by the year 2168.

Because the great majority of our immigrants come from Asian or Pacific nations, by the year 2031 about 30 percent of Canada's population will consist of what Statistics Canada calls visible minorities. South Asians currently make up 25 percent of those visible minorities, having recently surpassed Chinese Canadians, who make up 24 percent of the group. About 16 percent of Canada's visible minorities are black.

These new Canadians come to where there are jobs and where there are others like them, making migration patterns self-reinforcing. That is why, while 20 percent of Canada's population is foreign born—an astonishing figure, comparable to that of the peak migration periods around the turn of the last century—only 5 percent of Nova Scotia's population was born overseas. The figure is 11.5 percent for Quebec, but 28 percent for both Ontario and British Columbia. More than one person in four in

Canada's two largest English-speaking provinces was born overseas and is almost certainly Asian or some other variety of non-Caucasian. Keep out the Catholics? If only the Orange Lodge had known what was really going to hit them.

Because Canada is one of the world's most urban countries—the last decade in which the population was split 50–50 between urban and rural was the 1920s; today 70 percent of Canadians live in one of our 33 largest Census Metropolitan Areas (CMAs)—most immigrants migrate to cities. But they like some cities more than others: Toronto is 46 percent foreign born; Vancouver 30 percent; Winnipeg a respectable 18 percent; but Halifax only 7 percent.

This is why when you go through the agonies of security at Ottawa's Macdonald-Cartier Airport (Ottawa's foreign born population: 18 percent), the screeners are almost all white and speak English and French, while at Toronto's Pearson Airport or Vancouver International Airport the screeners are almost all brown, with a Babel of native tongues.

This should all have been wonderfully encouraging for the Liberal Party's twenty-first-century prospects. As long as new Canadians came here at a rate of a quarter million a year, adding a new Toronto to the country each decade, and as long as they remained loyal to the party that made this possible, the Liberals should have gone from strength to strength. Certainly that is what the Liberals themselves thought when Paul Martin fought so intensely for control of the party that he forced the resignation of the sitting prime minister, Jean Chrétien. He—it had always been a he—who controlled the Liberal Party controlled the country; so it had been, so it would always be.

Except it would not always be. The Liberals were reduced to a minority government in 2004; in 2006 they were forced into Opposition; in 2008 they did even worse; in 2011 they were reduced to a third-place rump. Where did all the votes go?

According to the Canadian Election Study, in the 2008 election the Liberals took 38 percent of the immigrant vote. The recently reunited Conservative Party under Stephen Harper, who formed its second minority government, took 33 percent. In other words, the Liberals had gone from owning 7 in 10 immigrant votes to fewer than 4 in 10 in the space of less than eight years. The Conservatives had gone from 1 in 5 to 1 in 3.

And in 2011? An informal survey of ridings in Ontario with unusually high populations of visible minorities tells the tale. Immigrant voters shifted heavily away from the Liberals to the Conservatives in the last election, the culmination of a trend that had been underway for a decade. The ridings shown in the following table, arranged from west to east, are all suburban ridings where new Canadians have put down roots.

2011 Federal Election Results in Ontario Ridings with High Populations of Visible Minorities

Riding	Immigrant population	Result
Brampton West	46%	Conservative gain from Liberals
Brampton–Springdale	47%	Conservative gain from Liberals
Bramalea–Gore–Malton	53%	Conservative gain from Liberals
Mississauga–Erindale	52%	Conservative hold
Mississauga–Streetsville	46%	Conservative gain from Liberals
York Centre	59%	Conservative gain from Liberals
Ajax–Pickering	31%	Conservative gain from Liberals

There is a contrarian explanation. Some analysts have argued that the immigrant vote didn't necessary shift to the Conservatives in 2011, at least not any more than it had already shifted. The Conservative vote didn't actually increase in many ridings, they point out. Instead, Liberal voters fled to the NDP. It was the rise in the NDP vote and decline of the Liberal vote that allowed the Conservatives to come up the middle and take the ridings, according to this argument. Immigrants may not have shifted their votes at all.

But we know that is not the case. During the 2011 election, the Conservatives devoted enormous resources to winning over immigrant voters in the Greater Toronto Area's so-called "905" ridings, named after their area code, and in Greater Vancouver. They advertised heavily in Cantonese, Mandarin, and Punjabi media. And they canvassed door to door in search of possible Conservative supporters, especially within the Chinese and Indo-Canadian communities. At least, that's what they were doing at the beginning of the campaign. Then they started to get the results of their private internal polls.[3]

The results were astonishing. One poll of voters in Toronto and Vancouver found that support in suburban ridings with large Cantonese-speaking populations for the Conservatives ranged from 55 percent to 70 percent. Chinese-Canadian voters overwhelmingly intended to vote Conservative. The word went out from the Tory war room to suburban riding campaign headquarters in Toronto and Vancouver: Stop bothering to identify Conservative supporters among Chinese voters. Just focus on getting every Chinese Canadian you can find to the polls. We'll take our chances on how they actually vote.

The Conservatives won their majority government and the Liberals were reduced to third place because immigrant Canadian voters in suburban ridings shifted their votes from the Liberals to the Conservatives. The election results suggest it, and internal political intelligence confirms it. The Conservative Party has become the party of immigrants.

For the people around that dinner table, puzzling over what had happened to their country—while Maurice slipped Gerald an illicit cigarette to calm him down—none of this made any sense. Immigrant voters living in the Greater Toronto suburbs, along with their counterparts in Vancouver, had joined with Prairie and rural Ontario voters to deliver a majority government to the Conservatives. The immigrants had voted with the Orange Lodge, or at least its political successors.

For the Laurentian elites it was entirely baffling. They were the descendants of those who had engineered Canada's immigration policy in the first place. They were the ones who revelled in the conglomeration of races and languages that the great cities had become. *They had made those cities possible.* Their children dated the children of Vietnamese and Filipino immigrants without a second thought; they ate cross-legged in restaurants, wolfing down things so raw and so spicy that their mothers would have fainted at the thought. They had fought for open immigration and abortion rights and multiculturalism and gun control and gay marriage and everything else that is right and good with Canada today. And the ones who should have been most grateful, the ones who should have identified most closely with the Canada that they had helped create, had turned away and sided with a party led by "thugs." How could this have happened?

2

The Great Divide

CONSERVATIVE VALUES AND THE BIG SHIFT

The 41st Canadian General Election is a fracture in time. Looking back, analysts will consider the years that came before it as part of one era, and the years that came after as part of another. Why? Because May 2, 2011, cemented the new Canadian politics.

The Laurentian elites are still in denial about the election. For them, it was an aberration, something reversible. It might even have been stolen, thanks to Tory chicanery—vicious ads, misleading robocalls, and who know what else? To get back in the game, the Liberal Party just needs to find the right leader and policy set. If they can't be found, then the NDP will have to be corralled. This Thomas Mulcair might be someone to do business with. The old playbook can still work, with a few carefully chosen substitutions.

They're wrong. The old playbook is worthless. Here's why.

Ruby Dhalla should never, ever have been defeated. Dhalla is a young, attractive Indo-Canadian from Winnipeg who had gained international attention when, as a student, she wrote to Indira Gandhi, urging her to resolve the tensions in the Punjab—a letter that the Indian prime minister quoted months before her assassination. A chiropractor and businesswoman who had opened up a chain of clinics across the GTA, Dhalla had also finished second in the Miss India Canada pageant of 1993. No wonder Paul Martin parachuted her into Brampton–Springdale—a large, ethnically diverse riding on the northwestern edge of Greater Toronto—in 2004. She won handily, with 48 percent of the vote, despite the objections of the local riding association, which favoured a local candidate.

She also won comfortably in 2006, but in 2008 her plurality slimmed to 41 percent, and in May 2011 she was whupped by Conservative candidate Parm Gill, who took 48 percent of the vote.

The Nannygate controversy, in which Dhalla was accused of mistreating domestic staff (nothing came of the accusations) might have had something to do with the loss. But the bigger problem for Dhalla, tactically, was that she and other Liberals in Toronto had failed to confront the Conservative strategy of using beachhead ridings to encroach on Liberal strongholds.

In the 2004 election, the new Conservative Party took

24 seats in Ontario, mostly in rural ridings. There was nothing surprising about that: rural Ontario had generally gone Conservative in elections; only the split between the Reform and Progressive Conservatives had allowed Jean Chrétien's Liberals to capture those seats in the nineties. Now that the Tories were once again united under Stephen Harper, it was natural that the rural ridings would join the opposition party's base.

But a few ridings on the rural/urban edge of Greater Toronto also went Conservative. One of them was Wellington–Halton Hills, which elected Michael Chong, a young IT professional who squeaked into the riding by just over 2,000 votes.

The party and Chong set out to entrench Conservative support in Wellington–Halton Hills, devoting the time and money needed to establish a strong constituency organization. That organization was evangelical—it spread the word to the surrounding ridings, where the Conservatives worked hard at recruiting candidates and beefing up their ground game.

Two of those adjacent ridings went Conservative in the 2006 election and became beachheads in turn. By 2008, the Tories had breached the Greater Toronto suburbs of Mississauga–Erindale, Thornhill, and Oak Ridges–Markham. Those new beachheads, in turn, helped propel the Conservatives into virtually complete control of the suburban ridings around Toronto, and even into the suburbs of Toronto itself in the last election. Ruby Dhalla was one of the victims.

Yet it would be wrong to attribute Conservative gains in suburban Ontario simply to tactical brilliance. There was also the Conservative message: Keep taxes low and the books balanced. Promote the military and crack down on criminals. Don't let government become hostage to environmental and other left-wing special interests. It was simple—Laurentianists would say simplistic—but it resonated, and not only with voters in the Prairies, the B.C. interior, and rural areas. It also resonated with suburban voters in Ontario, especially in the band of ridings that surrounds downtown Toronto. That breakthrough in the suburban GTA gave Stephen Harper his majority. And it did more than that.

We believe that the coalition between suburban Ontario voters and Western voters that propelled the Conservatives into a majority government represents a fundamental break with the political past. The cementing of this new coalition lies at the root of the eclipse of the Laurentian Consensus. For as long as this new coalition survives, Central Canadian elites will remain estranged from their traditional hold on power and control of the national agenda. We believe that this coalition could endure for a very long time. The Laurentian elites may never again be in charge. Just as the establishment of the American Northeast is now permanently in eclipse, with population and power flowing instead into the South and Southwest, so too the downtowns of Toronto, Ottawa, and Montreal may have been forever pushed outside the governing consensus. May 2, 2011, should be seen as a BC/AD divide.

But what caused this new divide? Polling data tell us the tale.

———————

In every election since 2006, Ipsos Reid has conducted extensive online election-day polls in collaboration with Global Television. As well as revealing how they voted, respondents also answered a 140-item questionnaire that probed their demographic backgrounds and their views on various topics. The poll offers a screen shot of exactly what voters were thinking and doing on election day.

The exit poll for the 41st general election captured the responses of nearly 40,000 people that included 2,689 self-employed voters, 1,394 voters from the gay and lesbian community, 6,551 residents of gun-owning households, 2,873 voters who described themselves as visible minorities, 1,502 teachers or professors, 145 farmers or fishers, 582 voters who said they were Aboriginal, 250 Muslims, 601 Jews, 228 Mennonites, 178 Caribbean immigrants, 192 construction workers, 79 members of the military, 7,855 advance-poll voters, and 8,991 voters who said they logged on to Facebook to discuss public policy and political issues. The data set is overwhelming.

And it reveals a profound shift in political identification among Ontario's suburban middle class, especially within the 15 ridings and 3 million people of the 905 area that stretches from Niagara Falls to Oshawa but excludes

Toronto. Traditionally, these voters identified their interests as those of middle-class voters in Toronto, led by the Laurentian elites. This is why, in most elections, ridings in the 905 have voted the same way as Toronto's 416.

But 905 voters have been known to shift their allegiance from the city to the country. It happened provincially in 1995 and 1999, when the 905 voted in solidarity with the 705, the mostly rural area code of central and northern Ontario, bringing to power and sustaining Mike Harris's Common Sense Revolution. It happened federally in the last election. Except in that case, Ontario's suburban middle class voted not only with their rural Ontario cousins, but with voters across the West. Fifty percent of those in the Greater Toronto Area voted Conservative, combining with 54 percent of voters in Manitoba, 56 percent in Saskatchewan, 68 percent in Alberta, and the 51 percent of British Columbia voters outside Vancouver.

In doing so, Ontario's suburban middle class left the Laurentian elites in their urban bastions of Toronto, Kingston (home of Queen's University), Ottawa, and Montreal isolated and impotent. It left Quebec, once again, outside government. Atlantic Canada's patchwork of support for all three parties contributed little to the overall result.

We know that the voters did this; the election results tell us that. The question is: Why? The answer is: The Conservatives convinced a plurality of voters in suburban Ontario that they shared the same values, values that were traditionally associated with rural voters or voters in the

Prairies. In other words, New Canada—suburban, immigrant, multicultural, middle class—found common cause with Old Canada—the white and often rural stock who are the descendants of the settler culture. They made common cause against the affluent, educated, liberal communities found in the downtowns of the big Central Canadian cities. The downtown elites thought they understood and spoke for the New Canada. May 2, 2011, proved conclusively that they didn't.

Patrick Muttart is a political marketing consultant who was Stephen Harper's principal secretary from 2006 to 2009. Within the Conservative Party, Muttart is credited with doing more than anyone other than Harper himself to put together the winning conditions for election victories. Muttart's great skill lies in identifying and targeting key voter segments. For him, the 2011 result was the culmination of years spent reaching out to those suburban Ontario voters by convincing them that the Conservative narrative was their narrative.

"In charting out a new course, a new national narrative, [the Conservative Party] is starting to move the country along with it," he said in a 2012 interview.[1]

The Conservatives' core message of low taxes, sound finances, and an overriding emphasis on growth, leavened with law-and-order values, had always found a loyal following in the West. The Conservatives' great achievement was to sell those same values to what Muttart calls "the suburbanization of affluence and influence."

In marketing terms, middle-class suburbanites are "strivers," upwardly mobile people seeking to own a home in a safe community while they pursue their dreams. They contrast with "creatives," who place a stronger emphasis on community supports, the environment, and international engagement. More likely to vote Liberal or New Democrat, creatives also tend to live downtown, which is where those parties remain strong, at least in English Canada. But in each election since 2004, suburban strivers have increasingly identified with the Conservatives—and immigrants are more likely to be strivers than creatives.

Harper's ability to appeal "to their aspirational sensibilities with the focus on jobs and growth and balanced budgets," as Muttart puts it, produced the Conservative victory of May 2011. Harper turned the Ontario suburban middle class into Conservative over-voters. Over-voters are people in a particular demographic group who disproportionately support one political party, as compared with the general public. So, for example, 40 percent of the population voted Conservative on May 2, but 72 percent of those in the military voted Conservative, according to the exit poll. So the military over-voted Conservative.

Who else over-voted Conservative? Old Canada, of course. They always have. White voters in rural areas overwhelmingly supported the Tories. Fifty-six percent of gun owners supported the Tories, as did 57 percent of self-declared Protestants. Seniors (54 percent of men and 52 percent of women over 65) voted Tory.

But not only Old Canada voted Conservative. Otherwise the party would still be in opposition, as its predecessor was throughout most of the twentieth century. Look at who else cast a blue ballot.

They spanned the classes: 50 percent of truck or bus drivers and 51 percent of people in management ranks voted Conservative. As we saw in the previous chapter, immigrants—a vital component of New Canada—joined the coalition. But not all immigrants. The Ipsos survey revealed that among immigrant Canadians who were eligible to vote, 45 percent who had lived in Canada for at least 10 years voted Conservative, while only 28 percent of those who had lived here for less than 10 years did so. This suggests that immigrants who are most likely to vote Conservative are those who have become well established economically, who have migrated out of the city core in search of the suburban dream of a garage, a big back yard, and maybe even a swimming pool.

While in some ways these voters are more socially conservative than other Canadians (85 percent of those who voted Conservative support the death penalty), in other ways they are not. Seventy-four percent disagreed with the statement "religious beliefs are important to how I voted."

What did these voters—urban and rural, immigrant and native born, blue collar and white collar—have in common? What made people across the country—from the rural riding of Prescott–Russell on the Ontario/Quebec border, to Brampton–Springdale, to every single riding in Calgary, to Vancouver Island North—all vote Conservative? Concern for the economy is the simple answer. Ninety-one percent of those who voted Conservative agreed with the statement: "I think it's important that the government maintain a balanced budget." Eighty-nine percent agreed that the economy should be the government's top priority. And this is the most crucial statistic of all: 62 percent agreed that "when the government gets involved in the economy, it does more harm than good."

This is the great shocking shift: Middle-class voters in suburban bastions surrounding Toronto and other Ontario cities allied themselves with rural Ontario voters, with rural and urban voters in the Prairies, and with rural and urban voters across B.C. (outside of downtown Vancouver) to elect a Conservative majority government because they all believed that the economy was the overriding issue facing the nation, and they trusted the Conservatives over the other parties to handle that issue. We should have set that sentence in bold face, italics, and capital letters, because this new values-based coalition is a fundamental component of the Big Shift.

Critics of the Conservatives may dispute whether voters were right to trust them on the economy; they may insist that other issues matter more than wrestling the deficit to the ground, or that it was the Conservatives who created those deficits in the first place. But what no one can dispute is that economic conservatism bound together the Conservative coalition in common cause.

The great recession of 2009 obviously had much to do with this. Liberals were once vaunted for their fiscal discipline, eliminating deficits in the 1990s and phasing in corporate and personal tax cuts after 2000. But the call for balanced budgets had originated within the Reform movement, and Conservatives were all about keeping government small and taxes low. After stumbling badly in the early days of the recession—Finance Minister Jim Flaherty didn't seem to know what had hit him—the Harper government recovered, launching an ambitious infrastructure stimulus package and a well-constructed bailout of General Motors and Chrysler, orchestrated in tandem with the Obama administration. As the recession ebbed, the Conservatives pivoted back to fighting the deficit while keeping taxes low and encouraging job creation through the private sector. The other parties simply couldn't, or didn't want to, put forward platforms and leaders who would outcompete the Conservatives on the economy. So the Conservatives got the most votes.

A Laurentian strategist shrugs. Maybe the Tories took the economy away from us, he thinks, but the economy won't always be the only issue. Once things settle down, other issues will emerge. People will start showing concern for the environment. They'll take an interest in what's happening overseas. The baby boomers especially will want to see new investments in health care and home care. They'll worry about whether Quebec might be getting ready for another referendum.

We don't think so. The recession of 2009 wasn't like other recessions. It revealed deep structural weaknesses in the economies of the developed world that nations are still grappling with, for the most part unsuccessfully. The United States appears to be only partway through a decade of downturn, as the debt accumulated by governments and consumers comes due. Southern Europe has entered a lethal spiral of unserviceable debt and uncompetitive economies that the European Union may not survive intact.

When emerging nations are urged to pour money into the International Monetary Fund—which was created to help those nations—so that the fund can now come to the aid of Europe, we know the legions truly are being recalled to Rome.

In this environment, the economy is not going to cede top spot any time soon. Managing it will be the standard by which governments at all levels will be judged. The Conservatives will be defeated when, and only when, another political leader and party convince voters they can do a better job on this all-important file.

Mind you, though the economy is top dog, it isn't the only dog. One other issue bound Conservative supporters together in the last election: crime. The Ipsos data show that "making communities safe from crime" served as an important differentiating role among voters. That is, while it was not a major factor in how people voted, crime did separate the parties and the leaders in the minds of voters—especially immigrant voters who had lived in Canada for a while.

Forty percent of voters picked Stephen Harper and the Conservatives as soundest choice on the issue of keeping streets safe from crime, followed by Jack Layton and the NDP (22 percent), and Michael Ignatieff and the Liberals (12 percent). Further analysis shows that the Conservatives' messaging worked best with immigrant voters (42 percent), who were more likely than the native born (39 percent) to see Harper and the Tories as strong on community safety. This was especially the case for immigrants who had been in the country for 10 years or more—44 percent picked Harper and the Tories as best on community safety. While the differences in these numbers may not seem big, they represent hundreds of thousands of votes and could very well have been decisive in ridings with lots of immigrants (such as around the outer GTA).

So New Canada and Old Canada made common conservative cause on two fundamental issues: jobs and crime. But although more people voted for the Conservatives than for any other party, more people voted for the other parties combined than for the Conservatives. What values did they vote for?

As everyone knows, the other great shocking shift of the May 2 election was the last-minute surge of Jack Layton's New Democrats to second place and Official Opposition, with 31 percent of the vote. The surge took place mostly in Quebec, where 43 percent of all voters cast ballots for the NDP, giving the party 59 seats and obliterating the Bloc Québécois. But of course, it wasn't just Quebecers who voted for social democrats. Forty-seven percent of gays and lesbians, 43 percent of Aboriginals, 43 percent of artists, 42 percent of women voters under 24, and 41 percent of students all stood by them. In other words, just about anyone who self-identified as a minority or an outsider inclined toward the NDP.

For many NDP voters, personality seemed to matter more than principle; fully 46 percent said they voted NDP mostly because *le bon Jack* was the leader. But it would be wrong to interpret what happened as simply a cult of personality. NDP voters were almost as likely as Conservative voters to support balanced budgets (85 percent) and to identify the economy as a top priority (75 percent). The difference is that 50 percent disagreed that the government does more harm than good when it gets involved in the economy. In other words, NDP voters worry about the economy just as much as Conservative voters, but they are more likely to look to government for help in hard times, while Conservative voters simply want government to balance the books and otherwise leave well enough alone.

As for the Liberals, who were reduced to 19 percent support, the party remained strong in parts of Atlantic Canada, particularly Prince Edward Island, and there were pockets of strength in downtown Toronto and Ottawa. Some immigrants remained loyal to the old party, which picked up 52 percent of the Muslim vote. And the Liberals remained attractive to many in the intelligentsia: 39 percent of those in the legal profession, 35 percent of those with a graduate degree, and 29 percent of artists voted Liberal. (If playwrights and political scientists elected governments, the Tories would have lost their deposit in most ridings.)

And while 84 percent of those who voted Liberal also agreed that balancing the budget was a top priority, a solid majority—56 percent—disagreed that the government does more harm than good when it mucks about with the economy.

We are in the midst of a troubled time when the rural, Prairie, Old Canada values of thrift, self-reliance, and paying as you go strongly appeal to many in the suburban immigrant New Canada as well. Suburbanites and recent Canadians also share a concern for safer streets and tougher laws to deter crime. They represent about 40 percent of the population.

Sixty percent think otherwise. Some worry more about social equity and environmental responsibility; others are deeply concerned about the economy but look to government to protect them from the worst of the consequences of the downturn. But their votes are divided between a social democratic party still in the process of retooling itself and a Liberal Party that has lost its way. The Laurentian elites have found no way to coalesce support among this inchoate, disgruntled mass of voters to defeat the Conservatives. Neither has anyone else.

That Laurentian political strategist perks up again. Clearly, all that's needed to unseat the Conservatives is to unite the majority of progressive voters across the country. The Liberals could still be resuscitated. The NDP could be tamed. The two could work co-operatively, competing against each other only in ridings where the Conservatives aren't already dominant. They could even formally merge.

We'll consider the Unite the Left argument further on. Here, though, we would observe only that the New Canada hasn't simply made common cause with the Old Canada; the Old Canada itself is becoming new again. Millions of voters are flooding west into the Prairies, lured by the promise of work in the oil industry and its affiliates. The Laurentianists find themselves squeezed by not one, but two forces: the values coalition between suburban Ontario *and* the West, and the shift of power and influence from the East and Centre *to* the West. Neither transformation works to their advantage.

Another thing handicaps those clinging to Laurentian assumptions: the disconnect between aspiration and expectation. For this we turn to a different pollster. In summer 2012, Nanos Research and the Institute for Research on Public Policy collaborated on an online poll of 2,000 Canadians that asked them to do two things: first, rate the importance of a series of major policy concerns; second, rate their expectation that governments (whether federal, provincial, or municipal) could make progress in addressing each concern.[2] The responses offer a powerful contribution to explaining why the federal Conservatives keep winning election after election, leaving the socially progressive parties and their Laurentian supporters defeated and dispirited.

Nanos-IRPP Policy Confidence and Importance Map

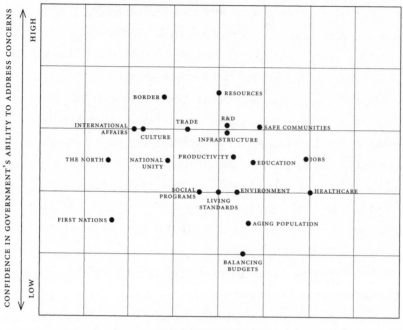

CONFIDENCE IN GOVERNMENT'S ABILITY TO ADDRESS CONCERNS

HIGH

LOW

BORDER ●

● RESOURCES

INTERNATIONAL AFFAIRS ●●

TRADE ●

R&D ●

CULTURE

● SAFE COMMUNITIES

INFRASTRUCTURE

THE NORTH ●

NATIONAL UNITY ●

PRODUCTIVITY ●

● EDUCATION

● JOBS

SOCIAL PROGRAMS ●

LIVING STANDARDS

● ENVIRONMENT

● HEALTHCARE

FIRST NATIONS ●

● AGING POPULATION

● BALANCING BUDGETS

MAJOR POLICY CONCERNS

LESS IMPORTANT

MORE IMPORTANT

As they always do, voters assigned the highest priority to improving the quality of public health care. They also put a strong emphasis on balancing government budgets and coping with an aging population. Nik Nanos calls these "transformative issues," in which voters are seeking major improvements to the society they live in and the governments they elect.

Yet when voters were asked how confident they were in the government's ability to find solutions to these high-priority problems, the majority had little confidence. Nanos dubbed this "public policy futility," in which people assign a high priority to transformative issues but have little hope that any politician of any stripe will make things better.[3]

Respondents placed a lower priority on what Nanos calls "transactional issues," incremental improvements that could make things modestly better. These include developing Canada's natural resources, policing the border, trading with other nations, and improving infrastructure such as roads and bridges. But on these issues, there was much greater confidence that governments could actually get something done.

There was only one issue that voters rated highly while also being reasonably confident that governments could tackle successfully: fighting crime.

You may have noticed something. The big transformative issues are embraced by socially progressive parties that rightly assume they are championing the values that matter most to voters. What they don't understand is that most voters have little confidence in their ability to deliver.

The more modest, transactional issues read like a Tory manifesto. The Harper government is all about making it easier to develop and sell natural resources; Stephen Harper and Barack Obama signed a border accord in 2012; the Conservatives are pursuing a plethora of trade deals in Europe and Asia; their economic recovery program focused on infrastructure spending. And of course, fighting crime is a signature issue for this government.

The Nanos/IRPP poll confirmed what the Ipsos Reid poll had already revealed: a sizeable portion of the public believes that governments do more harm than good when tackling the really big issues. What people realistically hope for are modest, incremental improvements: mowing the lawn rather than reseeding it or tearing it up. They can live with a few weeds.

As for the core priority of balancing the budget, there is only one way any government will convince a skeptical public: by balancing the budget.

What really handicaps the Laurentian Consensus when they confront these choices, making it impossible for them to fight back against the Tory tide, is that even when they discuss all this amongst themselves, they don't really understand what is happening. They don't feel it in their bones or in their gut. They don't, in short, get it. They especially don't get it in Quebec.

3

Quebec

THE SUN SETS. THE SUN MIGHT JUST POSSIBLY RISE.

Canada's first French-Canadian prime minister, Sir Wilfrid Laurier, was wrong when he predicted the twentieth century would belong to Canada. He should have said the twentieth century would belong to Quebec. Because it did, as far as this country was concerned. From the Conscription Crisis of the First World War to the near-death referendum in 1995, the great existential question for Canada was how to keep itself together by keeping Quebec, if not content, at least one shade shy of mutinous.

"What does Quebec want?" the Pearson generation asked itself. Answering that question dominated debates in Toronto and Ottawa and Montreal. West of Thunder Bay's Sleeping Giant mountain, the answer was: "Who cares?" But that response was intolerable to Central Canadians, and so the West was frozen out of the conversation. This was a Laurentian problem with which the Laurentian elites grappled, at times to the exclusion of all else.

Times have changed, and not because Quebec nationalism is on the wane. In fact, it may be resurgent, and that resurgence could once again pose a fundamental challenge for the Canadian union. The great difference, however, is what drives that nationalist wave today. For a generation and more, Quebec nationalism was powered by Quebec confidence. Those who sought separation believed that Quebec could exploit its abundant natural resources and its *dirigiste* model of economic planning to forge a confident, progressive, and sovereign nation that would finally erase the stain of defeat that General James Wolfe inflicted on this proud people.

Even those who believed Quebec's future would be more secure within Canada than without envisioned a federation anchored by the French fact. The language would be spoken from sea to sea; the federal government would fully reflect the social contract between English and French on which the country was founded; Quebec communitarian social values would temper, and ultimately trump, the laissez-faire brutalities of Anglo-Saxon Canada. The choice was a Canada without Quebec or a Canada dominated by Quebec.

Today, Quebec nationalism is rooted in fear. Fear among a population in relative, and perhaps one day in absolute, decline. Fear of an economic and political superstructure so distorted and unworkable that Quebec's dependence on subsidies from English Canada grows rather than weakens. Fear that, in their efforts to protect the French language and culture, Quebec's elites have rendered their society marginal—in the world, in Canada, perhaps even in Quebec itself.

Fearful nationalism can be a dangerous force. But it can also be a powerful tool. The dreams of some, especially in the West, that Quebec will somehow wither or evaporate will not be realized. Quebec still has a role to play in Canada, a powerful voice that must be heard. The province could yet become the anchor of a new political conversation. But it will do so from a very different demographic and political base than the one it enjoyed even a decade ago.

The election of May 2, 2011, was seismic not only because Stephen Harper's coalition of suburban Ontario and the West displaced the Laurentian Consensus. It was seismic because it disproved the axiom that no party could win a majority government at the federal level without substantial support from Quebec. Stephen Harper's majority included only five seats in the province. One of the new majority government's first acts was to pass legislation that redressed the increasing imbalance in the House of Commons. That imbalance protected rural ridings in small provinces at the expense of the growing urban powerhouses of Central and Western Canada. After much haggling, the final formula—Bill C-20, the *Fair Representation Act*—ensured that Quebec's representation in the House would never fall below the share to which it was entitled by its population. But although the province received three extra seats under the formula, those seats were swamped by the 15 that Ontario received and the six that went to both Alberta and British Columbia.

Quebec's slide in relative importance within the House of Commons reflects the province's ever-weakening gravitational pull. Quebec's influence over the rest of Canada is waning and will continue to wane for two simple reasons: population and language.

For many years, Quebec led Canada when it came to making babies. Some called it the "revenge of the cradle." Quebec's mothers would reverse the injustice perpetrated by General Wolfe on the Plains of Abraham in 1760; Anglophones might dominate in business, but they would never be the majority.

Actually, the truth is a bit more complicated. Quebec's birth rate was actually lower than Ontario's until about 1870. But then Ontario began to urbanize and modernize. Quebec stayed rural and economically backward. As a result, it moved ahead in the baby race. The all-powerful Roman Catholic Church condemned contraception, and Quebecers living in isolated farming communities looked upon more children as their way of bolstering the means of production.

Quebec's rush in the 1960s toward an urban and secular society was accompanied by a precipitous decline in its birth rate, which became so low that the Quebec government began offering incentives to women to have more children. Today, Quebec's birth rate of 1.74 children per woman of child-bearing age is slightly higher than the national average of 1.59 but well below the 2.1 needed to sustain the population. Like all other provinces, Quebec must rely on immigration. But while Quebec accounts for 23 percent of Canada's population, it accounts for only 19 percent of annual immigrants. No wonder the latest census revealed there are now more people in Western Canada than in Quebec and Atlantic Canada combined. In 2010, for example, 50 percent of immigrants to Canada came from Asia or the Pacific, with the emerging economic powerhouses of China and India two of the biggest source countries. In that same year, Quebec drew only 15 percent of its intake from Asia and the Pacific. Instead, 41 percent of new arrivals came from Africa and the Middle East, and 19 percent from the Caribbean and Latin America.

Many who immigrate to Quebec promptly leave. The Quebec government estimates that a paltry 10 percent of Investor Class immigrants selected by the province between 1999 and 2008 were still living there in 2010. And who can blame them? Quebecers face the highest tax rates in the country—fully 24 percent at the top marginal rate. Despite that crippling figure, provincial debt is 55 percent of gross domestic product. Quebec receives more than $7 billion annually in federal equalization payments, and more than $17 billion in total transfers from other provinces. Those total transfers equal one-quarter of the provincial government's total revenues.

And on top of all of that, 16 percent of Quebecers were over 65 as of 2011, according to the latest census data, compared with a national average of 14 percent. In other words, Quebec society is already getting older and more dependent on a shrinking base of working-age taxpayers to sustain a dangerously precarious fiscal situation. And instead of flooding the province with young, skilled immigrants from China and India, who could ease that demographic and fiscal crisis, the province is relying on a relatively small pool of candidates from less-developed source countries that include Algeria, Morocco, and Haiti, who could end up adding to the burden in the short term rather than easing it.

The result is a population that simply can't keep pace with the revenue needs of the Quebec government. This will inevitably force the province to depend even more on the rest of Canada for equalization payments and other transfers. How could a state in such a state ever realistically hope to strike out on its own? Cold economic calculation suggests the sovereignty movement is an exercise in deluded narcissism.

———

In the Saguenay each summer, local and imported actors and dancers gather to present a pageant describing the history of *Le Royaume,* as the region has long been called. One year, the reenactment of the Battle of the Plains of Abraham ended with Wolfe, mortally stricken, declaring "I die. But at least I have finally solved the language question."

The way we look at the world is shaped by the structure of our language. Language reflects and connects us to our home culture. Without realizing it, most of us are defined by language and powerfully—if unconsciously—attached to it. Language is personal.

That personal, passionate attachment to language can lead to confusion between what people wish for and what is. The Quebec government rightly and properly defends and advances the French language as a vital tool of preserving Québécois culture. The federal government, whatever party is in power, promotes the constitutional reality that Canada is a bilingual country. These are plain facts. Another plain fact is that anyone who wants to get almost anywhere today needs to speak English.

Ipsos is the third-largest market research company in the world, active in 85 countries and proudly headquartered in Paris. The co-presidents, Didier Truchot and Jean-Marc Lech, are both passionate advocates for all things French. However, when Ipsos decided to go global in the late 1990s, both men decided to make the working language of their company English. At the time, neither was proficient in the language. To this day, Jean-Marc doesn't speak more than taxi-cab English. Their reason for moving to English was not to accommodate the American market. At the time, Ipsos barely had any operations in the United

States. But English was the one language that most senior executives working in countries where Ipsos had offices could understand.

An example of how central English has become to this most French of French companies: at the annual meeting held in Buenos Aires in February 2012, which brought together representatives from the 67 countries where Ipsos operates, Jean-Marc delivered his speech by video in French, with English subtitles provided. The assumption was that everybody who needed to would be able to read his remarks in English, whatever their mother tongue.

Though the Europeans are loath to admit it, English has become the continent's lingua franca. On the day he was sworn in as president of France, François Hollande flew to Berlin to meet with German Chancellor Angela Merkel. But he was an hour and a half late because his plane had been struck by lightning.

"Sorry," he told her when they finally greeted each other, "My plane had a problem." The first words of the new French president to the German chancellor were in English.

It is sometimes jokingly said by Europeans that there are three kinds of English: the English a Czech uses when speaking with a Spaniard, which is standard English; the English that is spoken in the United States, which can be understood with difficulty; and British English, which is incomprehensible.

English has become the MS-DOS of the modern business world. That Microsoft computer operating system made global personal and business computing possible. English is doing the same for a globalized business community. Yes, it is still possible to have a successful local business career in a language other than English. But if the company you work for crosses borders, you probably can't have a leadership role unless you speak the new Latin.

A recent survey by Ipsos of workers from 26 countries showed that 27 percent of them had a job that required them to interact with people from other countries. Sixty-seven percent of people in that group used English for those interactions, even though 61 percent of them did not have English as a first language.

Employees from India (59 percent), Singapore (55 percent), Hong Kong (44 percent), and South Africa (42 percent) are the most likely to use English for cross-border communication. The exception is Latin America, where Spanish (or Portuguese, in the case of Brazil) are used. Only 3 percent of global workers use French for cross-border communication.

In Canada, 22 percent of workers have a job that requires cross-border communication. Four percent do it in French; 85 percent use English.

Things were not always this way. For centuries, French was the global language of diplomacy. Until 1929, the Geneva Conventions were published only in French. When the United Nations was founded in 1946, there were only two official working languages: English and French. There was a reason the Paris Peace Talks that ended the Vietnam War took place in Paris. Vietnam was a former French colony, and the educated elite of Vietnam spoke French. Paris was the city in which they felt most comfortable. Watch any documentary about the Vietnam War in which General Võ Nguyên Giáp, the hero of Dien Bien Phu, is interviewed, and you will hear him give his answers in beautiful Parisian French.

Today, the UN has six official working languages: Arabic, Mandarin Chinese, English, French, Russian and Spanish. And, unlike General Giáp, the world's economic and political elite no longer take their advanced education in any language other than English. According to the *Financial Times,* the top 10 business schools in the world are Stanford (U.S.), Harvard (U.S.), Wharton (U.S.), London Business School (U.K.), Columbia (U.S.), INSEAD (France/Singapore), MIT (U.S.), IE (Spain), IESE (Spain), and Hong Kong Business School (China). All of these, regardless of location, require applicants to have proficiency in English. The Spanish schools also offer MBAs in Spanish to local students, but they teach their international students in English. INSEAD, the top business school in France, teaches its international MBA students exclusively in English.

There was a time not that long ago when it was fashionable to insist that parents who wanted their children to be successful in the emerging global economy should ensure they learn Japanese or Mandarin. No more. The children of Japan and China are learning English instead. They learn it partly so that they can deal with America. But they learn it also so that they can deal with their counterparts in other countries. Don't believe us? Then attend a meeting of Chinese and French business executives without translators and watch how long it takes them to switch to English.

―――――――

In a profile entitled "What It Means to Be Canadian," the BBC recently observed, "Bilingualism, a political priority under the premiership of Pierre Elliott Trudeau in the 1960s and 70s, is a core element of the country's identity."

Actually, not so much. It's time to confront some plain truths about bilingualism in Canada. Let's start with a few statistics. According to the 2011 census, the mother tongue for 58 percent of Canadians is English. For 22 percent of Canadians it's French, and that represents a slight decline from 22.3 percent in 2006. The rest start out with something else. In their homes, 66 percent of Canadians speak English; 21 percent speak French; 13 percent speak neither.

The Office of the Commissioner of Official Languages reports that 13 percent of the population can speak French and nothing else. Sixty-eight percent speak only English. Seventeen percent are English/French bilingual. That, at least, is the number of people who identify themselves as bilingual. The number who could pass a test proving the claim is probably lower.

No wonder it's so hard to find a Supreme Court judge or an auditor general who speaks both languages. (The

Harper government got in trouble over both appointments.) If bilingualism is considered an absolute prerequisite for a job, only 17 percent of the population, at best, is available to be interviewed.

Among those who use more than one language at work—15 percent of the population—English is used most often by 78 percent; French by 22 percent. Outside Quebec, English is used in the workplace 99 percent of the time.

The size of the Canadian population has grown about 6 percent over the last six years, but the number of students in French/English immersion has grown by just over 10 percent. This is encouraging, but if the number of students in French immersion is steadily growing, why isn't the number of people identifying themselves as bilingual steadily growing also? (That 17 percent figure remains essentially unchanged from the proportion of Canadians who knew both official languages in 1996—18 percent.) One hypothesis might be that parents are selecting an immersive teaching environment for their children for reasons other than to teach them French. As *Globe and Mail* columnist Margaret Wente has observed: "People still enroll their children in French immersion, but not out of patriotic pride. Parents see it as a form of streaming, and a way to enhance their children's brains."[1]

Of course, it doesn't just matter how many Canadians are bilingual. It also matters how much bilingualism has entrenched itself in different parts of the country. For people promoting a bilingual Canada, these numbers are beyond disheartening. The following figures are provided by Canada's Commissioner of Official Languages. (The numbers of the territories are negligible, so they have not been included).

Percentage of French-Speaking Population in Canada (2006)

Canada	24 %
British Columbia	1.5%
Alberta	1.9%
Saskatchewan	1.6%
Manitoba	3.8%
Ontario	4.5%
Quebec	85.7%
New Brunswick	32.7%
Nova Scotia	3.6%
Prince Edward Island	3.8%
Newfoundland and Labrador	0.4%

With the exception of Quebec and New Brunswick, less than 5 percent of the population of any province speaks French.

So, what does it cost us to maintain the fiction of being a bilingual country? A report released in January 2012 by the Fraser Institute shows that Canada's 10 provinces spend nearly $900 million annually providing bilingual government services.[2] Including the $1.5 billion the federal government spends on bilingualism, Canadian taxpayers are footing an annual bill of $2.4 billion for bilingual services, at a cost of $85 per person.

Where does this leave Canadians and Quebecers? If you want to have a national or global career in Canada today, you cannot do it in French. It must be in English. The only meaningful place (other than Quebec) where speaking French now counts in career terms is in Ottawa, working within the federal government. Even then, the expectation is that you will be able to function as well in English.

This state of affairs leads to a worrying estrangement between the federal public service and the rest of the country. The great majority of bilingual Canadians hail from what is known as the "bilingual belt"—the communities close to the Ontario/Quebec and the New Brunswick/Quebec borders. Happily for the Laurentian Consensus, this is its home turf as well. The bilingualism requirements in the federal public service ensure that most mandarins will come from and be part of the Laurentian elites.

But as the elites' political influence wanes, with few of the hundreds of thousands of immigrants arriving annually having an interest in or aptitude for French, and as the economic and political power of the West grows, the federal public service becomes more and more unlike the public that it serves and that it is supposed to represent. The mandarinate come from and look to a Canada that no longer exists. They too often ignore the rest of the country, which is increasingly most of the country. And the rest of the country ignores them. No wonder Ottawa has never seemed less relevant in the eyes of most Canadians. A July 2012 Ipsos Reid poll revealed that 84 percent of Canadians believe the political elite in Ottawa is out of touch with the needs and values of average Canadians.

What's happening to Quebec is mostly beyond its and Canada's control. Shifting global immigration patterns and the rise of English as the default language for international business are pushing the province ever further toward the periphery of Canada, North America, and the world. The combination of economic globalization, low birth rates, and inadequate population replenishment with the right type of immigrants has painted *la belle province* into a very tight corner. If these trends aren't reversed, Quebec will increasingly become a province of old, white pensioners without the means to pay for their coveted social programs, protecting a language that fewer Canadians or global citizens will understand.

Rather than belling the cat and talking about the real issues facing Quebec, the Laurentian elites have instead decided to condemn Ottawa for giving up on reconciling the two nations, especially since Stephen Harper and the Conservatives came to power. Witness the interview that former Liberal Party leader Michael Ignatieff gave to the BBC. Ignatieff declared that "the emotional bonds that once existed between French and English Canada are all but gone . . . we don't have anything to say to each other any more . . . there's kind of a contract of mutual indifference, which is very striking for someone of my generation." On

Quebec independence, Ignatieff opined, "I think eventually that's where it goes."[3]

The national media and the political class were furious. The Liberal Party was particularly incensed that its former leader seemed to be giving up on the union. Ignatieff quickly recanted. Galileo recanted too. But what is said cannot be unsaid.

The Laurentian elites, who despise Stephen Harper for being beyond their pale, forget that, in one crucial respect, he once tried to be one of them. When he first took office, Harper looked to woo Quebec. He believed it was the only way he could win his majority. As such, he became more Brian Mulroney or Joe Clark than Preston Manning. He tried to fix the "fiscal imbalance" in Canada by shovelling money into Quebec, and declared that the Québécois were a "nation" within a united Canada. He even granted Quebec its own delegate at UNESCO. His reward was to be reduced to five seats in the province in the last election.

Just as Quebec gave up on him, so too Stephen Harper seems to have given up on Quebec. Since winning their majority government, the Conservatives have begun stripping equalization components from programs such as health transfers, which does no favours to the province that is the largest recipient of equalization. The Tories waved a red flag at the Quebec bull by putting the designation *Royal* back in the navy and air force; it had been removed partly to assuage Quebec's anti-monarchy sensibility. Cutting funding to the CBC was seen in Quebec as a hostile move; Radio-Canada is a vital cultural voice within the province. Scrapping the gun registry offended the province that spurred its creation after the terrible shootings at the École Polytechnique in 1989. And Quebecers, who consider themselves environmentally enlightened thanks to their reliance on hydroelectricity over carbon-based sources, howled at the Tories' decision to withdraw from the Kyoto Protocol.

As the *Globe and Mail*'s Jeffrey Simpson has correctly observed, "Quebec is completely estranged from the Harper government, and the estrangement is reciprocated. Stephen Harper is seen in Quebec as Pierre Trudeau used to be in Alberta, and the Conservative Party that once had hoped for a breakthrough in the province is discredited."[4]

This estrangement led many observers within Quebec to fear a revival of separatism, as the province became ever more distant from Ottawa and the Parti Québécois awaited its inevitable return to power. Those fears became acute in autumn 2012, when Parti Québécois Leader Pauline Marois eked out a narrow victory over Jean Charest's discredited Liberals and François Legault's upstart Coalition Avenir Québec. With scarcely a third of the popular vote, with a strong opposition, with her own caucus riven by conflict between hard-line separatists and others who simply wish to govern, and with polls showing that less than a third of the population would vote Yes in a referendum on sovereignty, the prospects of such a referendum being held within the foreseeable future appear bleak.

Nonetheless, the PQ may one day be optimistic enough, or desperate enough, to hold yet another vote on secession. If so, the fight over whether Quebec should become a sovereign nation will differ from previous contests. The battles of the past were driven by an ascendant, vibrant Quebec culture and baby boomers at the peak of their intellectual and earning powers. These Quebecers had a strong desire to create a new voice in the world. The challenge was met by Laurentian elites, who saw the struggle to answer and contain Quebec's aspirations as the fight of their lives. If there is another wave of nationalism in Quebec, it will be very different from the waves we experienced in 1980 and 1995. It will be about defending what once was and trying to keep pace with a country dominated by Toronto, the West, and Stephen Harper's new political coalition. Quebec nationalists will be playing defence, not offence.

In our view, another referendum is unlikely, and if there is one, the separatists probably won't win. But Quebec will go its own way, whether it wants to or not. It is doing so many things wrong, and its influence is declining so fast, that no other future is possible. Quebec risks turning into Canada's version of Greece, in which it defensively withdraws from the Canadian project and becomes an economically untenable alternate universe—a French-speaking, fiscally challenged society of delusion. Even more challenging for the unity of the federation is the fact that Canadians outside Quebec are increasingly indifferent to whether it stays or goes. A June 2012 Ipsos Reid poll revealed that 49 percent of Canadians outside Quebec "don't really care" if the province separates.

These are difficult ideas to contemplate, but they need to be discussed if we are truly to understand the future direction of Canada. And they need to be discussed without an eye to easy, politically predictable conclusions and prejudices. For every *pur laine* sovereigntist who sees Quebec as having a bright, independent future guaranteed by the province's abundant natural resources, there's a Canadian somewhere else who just wishes Quebec would go away. The right and real discussion is about the relentless twin forces of economic globalization and demographics and what they really mean for Quebec's (and Canada's) future.

And who will lead this discussion for Quebec? It certainly won't be the cast of Quebec characters that we all know so well. Their nationalist leadership is geriatric. Even the "coquette" of the sovereigntist movement, Louise Beaudoin, was born in 1945. Current PQ leader Pauline Marois was born in 1949. Godfather of the movement Jacques Parizeau is in his eighties, and the spiritual leader of the last wave of separatism, Lucien Bouchard, is in his mid-seventies. Gilles Duceppe is in his sixties. Let's not even mention the Quebec Liberal Party, which has been so tainted with allegations of corruption that its defeat in the 2012 provincial election could well be a step down the road to its eventual extinction.

While only Quebecers can solve the internal economic contradictions they have imposed on themselves—

prodded, perhaps, by the bond rating services—on the national political stage there remains a tantalizing possibility, one that offers Quebec a new and very different way to participate in Canada's national life. There could be another future for Quebec that keeps it embedded firmly within Canada. As the *Toronto Star*'s Chantal Hébert has observed: "As Quebec disengages from the constitutional front, the issues that mobilize its activists also increasingly have legs in the rest of Canada."[5] We saw this scenario start to take shape during the 2011 federal election, and also in the student protests that rocked the province during the spring of 2012. In this possible future, Quebec becomes the anchor for an emerging national progressive coalition that runs from the province through the downtowns of the major English-Canadian cities, and in communities hurt by the policies of the governing Conservatives.

Let's quickly remind ourselves of what's at stake here. The current values and priorities of the Harper government emphasize a tough approach to law and order that punishes criminals and rewards gun owners, that plays up Canada's connection to the monarchy as well as other elements of the British colonial past, that is pro-military and anti-peacekeeping, that takes the side of Big Oil, that considers the CBC and other cultural institutions elitist and contemptuous of conservative values, that minimizes the role of the federal government in redistributing income and enforcing national standards for social programs, including health care.

Just listing that agenda suggests its polar opposite: giving new life to the federal power as a means of enforcing equity both vertically, among classes, and horizontally, among regions; protecting and advancing a national culture that spans regions and languages; reviving a vision of Canada than transcends its colonial past; promoting a pan-national strategy for renewable energy. That might be something worth voting for.

Who will galvanize that progressive alternative to the current conservative orthodoxy? Will it be the newly ascendant NDP, a revived Liberal Party, or an amalgam of the two? We will discuss later what that political alternative might look like. But we already know from where it could come: it could come from Quebec, which remains the last bastion of progressive solidarity in Canada.

From Quebec could come the invitation to the suburban Ontario middle class to abandon its alliance with the conservative Pacific West and embrace a progressive Central Canadian future. From Quebec could come a new alliance within the manufacturing heartland combining against the resource-based hinterlands. From Quebec in conjunction with Ontario could come the twenty-first-century equivalent of Robert Baldwin and Louis-Hippolyte Lafontaine.

Or not. The challenges to that coalition would be formidable. It would require Ontario voters to see in Quebecers a more realistic reflection of their political selves than they find in the West. It would require a declining, ever more isolated province to re-emerge as a politically engaged, even dominating, pillar of a reconstructed political establishment. It would mean handing Canada back to the Laurentian elites, even though those elites have been increasingly discredited in election after election.

Still, the progressive response to the conservative coalition must eventually emerge somehow, and from somewhere. A party and a leader will one day challenge the Harper hegemony.

And despite the overwhelming evidence of Quebec's demographic, economic, and linguistic decline, that leader's accent just might be French.

4

It's Not ROC Anymore

THE OTTAWA RIVER CURTAIN DESCENDS

"We must love one another or die," W.H. Auden warned. But in Canada, sometimes it's difficult to find the love. There is so much country, and there are so few of us, that each cluster withdraws into its own solitude. And there are so many solitudes. Apart from language, there really isn't much that makes Quebec society that much more distinct than Newfoundland's, or Nunavut's, or Calgary's for that matter. We're like the United States in that respect—so many disparate cultures inhabiting one political space that sometimes it's hard to understand how we keep it together. The answer, of course, is that both countries have federal systems of government, allowing each region to go its own way in local matters, bound with the others in common cause only on the great national issues.

For the Laurentian elites, this wasn't enough. They hoped that a broadcasting network here, an arts grant there, a national social program, or a railroad or a highway would bind us all together. The railroad certainly helped, but it was built well over a century ago. Public health care seems to have taken root, along with a certain fondness for the Charter of Rights and Freedoms. But for the most part, each region of the country still goes its own way.

And we're going to go our own way a lot more than we used to. As with so much else that we talk about in this book, it doesn't matter whether you consider this a good thing or a bad thing. What matters is that you understand it's a thing. Laurentian conventional wisdom divided Canada between French and English, between Quebec and the ROC (the dismissive Laurentian acronym for the Rest of Canada). But there is a new, even more powerful divide emerging: between poor and rich, between declining and growing, between past and future. The dividing line runs from the southern tip of James Bay to just west of Montreal. We call it the Ottawa River Curtain.

The Atlantic Canadian Reality Distortion Field

Flush with a majority government, with the opposition weak and divided, and with the books dangerously out of balance, the government of the day decided to tackle unemployment insurance. We're talking Jean Chrétien in the nineties, not Stephen Harper in the 2010s. The Liberal reforms were not that different from the current Conservative ones: seasonal workers (primarily in the Atlantic provinces) who were chronically dependent on Unemployment

Insurance during the many months when they weren't working would see their benefits cut back. The goal was to lessen dependence and encourage year-round jobs. The result was a spanking: the Liberals lost 20 seats in the region in the 1997 election. The reforms were quickly scrapped. The only change that remained was that Unemployment Insurance became Employment Insurance—your federal government at work.

In the early days of the proposed reforms, the government hired Darrell Bricker and his Ipsos (then Angus) Reid Group to conduct a series of focus groups throughout Atlantic Canada on the proposed UI changes. Focus groups are structured discussions with 10 to 12 randomly recruited people from a local community. Bricker led the discussions, which were typically held in rooms with one-way glass so that the groups could be viewed by the client (in this case, government officials) without disturbing the conversation. In smaller communities, side-by-side rooms in local hotels were used.

The focus groups revealed that Atlantic Canadians have what might be called a unique approach to economic theory. For example, it became obvious very quickly that the ordinary folks who were there to talk about Unemployment Insurance reform were intimately familiar with the rules of the program—what you needed to qualify for benefits, how much you could expect to get—but not much interested in considering where the money came from. To them, unemployment insurance was a particularly generous form of car or house insurance: you paid your premiums every month, and in exchange you were entitled to collect your benefits every year.

To test the resilience of this attitude, Bricker introduced notions taken from a list put together by policy experts. He asked members of the group how much they paid into UI each year, and how much they collected in benefits. The premiums were typically in the hundreds, and the benefits in the thousands. He would then ask: "Does this seem fair and reasonable to you?" While briefly knocked off stride by such a question, the focus group members recovered quickly, insisting that insurance was insurance, regardless of the relationship between premiums and benefits.

"Let me get this straight," Bricker would press them. "You pay the same premium as everybody else in the country, you collect much more in benefits than the premiums you pay, and you expect to do this every year. Does this make any sense to you?" After some back and forth, they would generally agree that, yes, it made perfect sense.

Bricker would then introduce a comparative worker. "Imagine the life of an individual who lives in Oakville, Ontario," he would say. "He or she commutes a couple of hours every day to work and back. They get a few weeks a year of vacation. They pay the same UI premiums as you, but they never collect benefits. Do you think it's fair that they are asked to pay for somebody down here who collects every year?" For a few moments, the members of the group would look down at the floor. But invariably, someone would pipe up with something like: "That's what it means to be a Canadian. Those who can afford to pay, pay, and those who need the benefit collect it. That's the Canadian way." Karl Marx couldn't have put it any better.

Almost 20 years later, nothing has changed. In the 2012 budget, the Conservatives introduced changes to EI that require seasonal workers to travel to take jobs, and to accept work at a lower wage or in another field, or risk losing benefits. The proposals were greeted with outrage in Atlantic Canada, where the Conservatives can now expect to win few if any seats in the next election. This time, too, the feds convened focus groups before announcing the reforms. Those conducting the sessions reported a peculiar mindset among seasonal workers, who seemed not to understand that EI made it possible for them to live in communities where there were no full-time jobs. "When the question of whether EI rules or 'generosity' affect thinking about moving, the usual reaction from participants was a blank stare, as most did not consciously relate the two," the report concluded.[1]

These studies capture perfectly what we call the Atlantic Canadian Reality Distortion Field. It's a place where facts go to die, where the laws of economics are miraculously suspended, and where a universal belief system is founded on the universal denial of reality. Only in Atlantic Canada—and in a few select remote sections of other provinces—would anybody suggest that it's perfectly reasonable to work in a "seasonal industry" with the expectation that you get to work part of the year, and then the government takes over from the employer for the rest of the year while you do nothing—at least, nothing above the table. Only in Atlantic Canada would it be universally accepted that this should never, ever change.

What do we mean when we say "universal"? The Atlantic premiers called a press conference in June 2012 to protest the Harper government's EI rule changes. Prince Edward Island Premier Robert Ghiz patiently explained some economic fundamentals to what he clearly thought were rather dim-witted voters and politicians down the road. "Central Canadians, all Canadians, like to enjoy our lobster, our french fries, our mussels, our oysters, but they have to realize that these are all seasonal in nature," he explained, as the distortion field hummed quietly in the background. "So we need the federal government to be able to realize that one size does not fit all across our country."[2]

If there are to be potatoes in Toronto, there must be wage subsidies for Prince Edward Island. No pogey, no potatoes.

New Brunswick NDP MP Yvon Godin, raging against Conservative perfidy, made the same point at a forum in Ottawa that spring. While John Ibbitson listened slack-jawed, Godin argued with Acadian passion that without subsidies for Maritimers there would be no lobster fishery, and no lobsters for anyone in Ontario to eat.

Outside the distortion field, fundamental laws of supply and demand ensure that, even without subsidies, potatoes and lobsters are available at a market-clearing price in places as far from their source as Toronto. It might even be possible to get them in Winnipeg.

Back inside the distortion field, politicians, fishers, and union leaders warn that, without the federal subsidies, family-owned businesses will be displaced by giant international corporations that will swoop in, buy up the licences, force governments to scrap legislation designed to protect local businesses and seasonal workers, and replace the whole thing with some monstrous alternative based on privately generated wages and profit. Another name for this horror is capitalism.

Don't blame Atlantic Canadians for being trapped within this distorted perspective. The Laurentian Consensus created it by emphasizing national unity over economic reality. The mindset goes all the way back to John A. Macdonald and the National Policy, which protected manufacturers in Ontario against foreign competition. The fishing industry is simply a vestige of this ancient mercantile system. While most of the rest of the country has shaken off the thrall of protectionism and subsidies—even Liberals ultimately, if reluctantly, embraced the free trade agreements with the United States and Mexico—Atlantic Canada remains trapped within it, which may be why it was the only region of the country that largely remained loyal to the Liberals in the last election, and where the last remnants of the Progressive Conservatives, such as Peter MacKay, can still be found.

The exit poll run by Ipsos Reid on election day shows

why. While Atlantic Canadians shared the view with the rest of the electorate that the economy was the primary issue in the country, they preferred the "Family Pack" of spending solutions offered by the Liberals to the austerity diet proposed by the Conservatives. And why not? After all, government already offers them a lifestyle to which they have long been accustomed but for which they don't have to pay. Who wouldn't want more of such a good thing?

It boils down to values. A Harper-friendly conservative sees government as part of the problem, not the solution. For Atlantic Canadians, the state is more likely to be seen as the only solution. Understandable, since in Atlantic Canada the state is a miraculous creature that provides vastly more in services than it receives in taxes.

Federal Transfers as a Proportion of Provincial Budget[3]

Province	Federal transfer	% of provincial budget
Alberta	$3.7 billion	12.2
Ontario	$19.5 billion	19.4
New Brunswick	$2.5 billion	36.8
Nova Scotia	$2.9 billion	32.1

But the Atlantic Canadian Reality Distortion Field is weakening and may soon collapse. The four provinces are rapidly aging—people over 65 make up roughly 16 percent of the population versus a Canadian total of 14.8 percent—and none is doing a decent job of attracting immigrants.

Immigrant Population of Atlantic Canada in 2006

Province	% of Canada's population	% of Canada's immigrants
New Brunswick	2.3	0.4
Prince Edward Island	0.4	0.1
Nova Scotia	2.9	0.7
Newfoundland and Labrador	1.6	0.1

That is what demographic decline looks like. The Atlantic Canadian Reality Distortion Field is destroying what is left of the local economy, and the result is a slow-motion population collapse. Occasionally, you will find a politician who worries about this. Usually, he or she will call for federal aid to combat it.

There are beacons of hope. Newfoundland's oil industry, coupled with the enormous potential of Labrador hydro, is building a new, skilled workforce in that province; the recent announcement of the shipbuilding program for Canada's navy offers tremendous possibilities for attracting skilled workers to Halifax. And if an educated population is an economy's most important asset, then the Maritimes should be thriving, thanks to its network of excellent universities.

But for the seasonal workforce, for industries that casually count on government to look after their workers for half of the year, the future is bleak. The old economy is doomed by an aging population and by too few immigrants. Atlantic governments talk about bringing in newcomers and jump-starting renewal, but their efforts are invariably half-hearted, they invariably fail, and they invariably end with an appeal to Ottawa for more assistance.

And though the distortion field blinds most Atlantic Canadians to this new truth, the reality is that the collapse of the Laurentian Consensus must also bring about the collapse of the relentless predictability of transfers from west to east. The day will soon come when the Oakville worker downs tools when it comes to supporting PEI fishers. Already rebellion is in the air.

Ontario Is Manhattan; Ontario Is Ohio

For more than a century, Ottawa and Ontario had a compact that guaranteed Canada's central province would always be its most populous and powerful. That compact is broken. Imperial Ontario has lost its empire. Loyal Ontario no longer has reason to be loyal. Prosperous Ontario is under threat. Liberal, Laurentian Ontario is on the wane. Conservative, Pacific Ontario is on the rise.

There is a reason that middle-class suburban voters have increasingly supported the Conservatives in every election since 2004. The reason is wheat.

Most Canadian provinces consist of a hub city surrounded by hinterland. Montreal is the hub of Quebec; Halifax of Nova Scotia; Winnipeg of Manitoba; Vancouver of British Columbia; Edmonton and Calgary of Alberta, and so on. Only Southern Ontario is built on a grid of roads connecting villages, towns, and cities more or less evenly distributed from Windsor to Cornwall.

As the Liberal MP and economist John McCallum[4] wrote more that 30 years ago, the soil there is so fertile and the climate so, well, not awful, that the first settlers got rich selling wheat to hungry Britain during and after the Napoleonic wars. The rivers and streams provided the falls and rapids that powered the grist mills that ground the wheat, which is why so many towns in southern and central Ontario were built beside rivers. The Industrial Revolution turned those grist mills into factories and Ontario into the economic engine of Canada, with almost 40 percent of its population and GDP. Wheat made Ontario wealthy, and wealth made Ontario confident. But hard times and lost jobs have shaken that confidence. Ontario voters—at least, suburban middle-class Ontario voters—support the Conservatives because (though they might not be aware of the historic details) they are afraid they might be losing their empire, the empire that was founded on wheat.

In the early years of this country, when Ontario reigned supreme, Queen's Park and Ottawa made a deal. The federal government would protect Ontario's interests by throwing up tariff barriers that forced consumers in other provinces to buy Ontario products. Toronto banks would dominate finance. Roads and rail and, ultimately, air travel would link east and west to centre. Ontario would be the imperial heart of Confederation; the Western provinces would be little more than colonies.

And Toronto would be the imperial capital, part of an imaginary (because only Canadians imagined it) triangle that had New York and London as the other fixed points. Toronto would be the country's cultural centre, home to the big publishing houses and broadcasters. It would have the biggest and best university. If anyone in Canada ever came up with a new idea, they would come up with it in Toronto.

In exchange for centrality, Ontario would sacrifice identity. To be an Ontarian—a word no one uses, because it has so little meaning—was to be a Canadian. Ontario would share its wealth with the poorer regions of the country through the equalization program, because Ontario had so much to give. Ontario would consent to being underrepresented in the House of Commons, because it had enough of the power that mattered not to care. Let the other parts of Canada nurse their local accents and particular grievances. Ontario would serve the national interest, because it *was* the national interest.

This was the first, and possibly greatest, of the Laurentian contracts, the one that bound Ontario to the other English-Canadian provinces and they to it. They would be the market, Ontario the seller. They would sign their mortgages with Toronto banks, buy cars made in Windsor and Oshawa, listen to news broadcasts from Toronto newsrooms, ultimately receive their baby bonuses or equalization cheques courtesy of Ontario taxpayers. The contract, of course, was negotiated in Ontario among Ontario elites. Everyone else was simply asked to sign on the dotted line. Most had little choice. They needed the money.

Ontario premiers would sometimes chafe at the synchronicity between Ottawa and Ontario. As the chief representatives of the provincial government, they had their own concerns: Toronto groaned under the influx of newcomers and needed billions to upgrade roads and public transit; the Ontario economy competed with that of the Great Lakes states, whose voters have an enormous influence on the outcome of presidential elections. To attract investment, Ontario needed to offer incentives that sometimes only Ottawa could provide. And as the feds built equalization components into each and every national program, from health care funding to national research chairs, Ontario premiers demanded that more of the money stay at home, where it was needed.

But as the political scientist David Cameron has observed, an Ontario premier is "like a general without an army. He can climb on his horse and ride to Ottawa and pound the table and say what he needs. But where are the troops? The feds know where the troops are. They're back home, voting for them, and thinking about the national interest, and assuming somehow Ontario's concerns are going to be met."[5]

The premier of New Brunswick speaks for New Brunswick; the premier of Alberta for Alberta; the premier of Quebec for the Quebec nation. But who does the Ontario premier speak for? With more than 100 MPs in the House, and with a majority of those MPs most likely on the government's side—otherwise, it wouldn't have the seats needed to win government—prime ministers could and did dismiss Ontario premiers, since the same people who voted for one had voted for the other, and Ottawa had easily as great a claim on the Ontario's voter's affections as Queen's Park.

No more.

The Democratic Party strategist James Carville once described Pennsylvania as a state with "Philadelphia on one end and Pittsburgh on the other, and a whole lot of Alabama in between." The economic shocks of globalization and recession have turned Ontario into a province with a little bit of Manhattan surrounded by a whole lot of Ohio. And Ohio is restless.

————

Toronto can be ugly: squat houses, mostly indifferent commercial architecture, an aborted waterfront, and no central park. Decades of municipal politicians who were at best mediocre and at worst crazy, coupled with provincial and federal governments that could score political points elsewhere—anywhere, actually—by thumbing their noses at Hogtown, have left the city roads crumbling and public transit a full generation behind current demand. And the sprawl is godawful: tract housing, arterial roads, and shopping malls stretching 100 kilometres in every direction, with every kilometre looking just like every other kilometre and all of it a downtown elitist's nightmare.

And yet Toronto is the world's most exciting city. This is not because its theatre surpasses London's or its publishing houses outshine New York's—because they don't, not by a long shot. Its music scene is good but not great; its museums and galleries are second tier. Its universities range from mediocre to admirable, but none approach the best American schools.

Toronto is the world's most exciting city because it is ground zero in the multicultural experiment: the place on earth where more people from more places live together than anywhere else on earth.[6] These people are the engine of the city's cultural vibrancy. They are what connects it to the world. They are the final proof that immigrants don't take jobs from the native-born; they create jobs for them.

Services drive the Greater Toronto region's economy: 6 million people take in one another's washing. Not many people make anything there any more, but the financial services sector is strong; the cultural industries have never been this vibrant; everyone sells this, markets that, or consults; every other storefront is a restaurant. Unemployment has been running higher than the national average and the housing bubble is always a pinprick away from calamity. But despite every challenge—did we mention the crazy mayors?—Toronto is alive and growing and thriving and plunging into this century with a grin.

Outside the city, and its suburbs and exurbs, it's a different story. Three hundred thousand manufacturing jobs have disappeared in Ontario. Globalization is part of the problem; the recession was part of it; the strong dollar is part of it too. Some stars flamed: Research in Motion used to be Apple; now it's Nokia.

The factories by the rivers where the grist mills used to be now sit empty. Ambitious developers have turned some of them into condominiums, where there is demand, or converted them to stores and offices. Others just slowly fall down. The American automakers have recovered from their near-death experience, but by retooling with fewer jobs and lower wages. Right to Work states south of the border are luring companies away with promises of lower wages and no strikes. Unemployment rates in Ontario have been above the national average since June 2006. Its population growth rate has dropped below the national average, according to the 2011 census. The province took in 100,000 fewer immigrants between 2006 and 2011 than it did between 2001 and 2006. The McGuinty government's efforts to promote alternative energy that would, in turn, develop a new energy industry through research and investment left the province with skyrocketing electricity bills and staggering debt—and not much to show for it.

Ontario is turning into a Springsteen song.

This wasn't supposed to be part of the deal. The deal was that the heartland would grow ever richer, and then send the money to the provinces that needed it. But Ontario has become just another region. David MacKinnon, a former senior public servant in both the Nova Scotia and Ontario governments who also served as CEO of the Ontario Hospital Association and the Ontario Development Corporation, has studied the equalization system extensively. He observes that Ontario taxpayers—who pay twice as much into equalization as the province receives from the program—endure lower levels of public services than those in receiving provinces.

There are twice as many federal bureaucrats, as a share of the overall population, in Prince Edward Island as in Ontario, even though that is where the national capital is. The island also has three times as many provincial bureaucrats, on a per-capita basis, as well as 50 percent more nurses, 28 percent higher university funding, and twice as many long-term care spaces.

Twenty-six percent of the Manitoba and Nova Scotia labour force is employed in the public sector. In Ontario the figure is 18 percent. Both Manitoba and Quebec subsidize electricity consumption, MacKinnon points out. Ontario taxpayers help pay for those subsidies.

In fact, over the past 50 years, MacKinnon calculates, Ontario has on average contributed 4 percent of its gross domestic product to support other provinces. This is roughly the same percentage of GDP that the United States spends on defence, and the U.S. over the past 50 years has been at war more often than not.

"Viewed from this perspective, the impact of the regional subsidy effort on Ontario is like fighting a 50-year war," MacKinnon observed in an October 2012 speech.

Everyone suffers: Ontario is less able to compete with other manufacturing-based economies that don't see a sizable portion of their GDP drain away to other jurisdictions. Receiving provinces pay, too, through subsidy distortions that undermine the private sector. Ganong Bros. Limited, the New Brunswick confectionary company, must import Romanian workers to keep its factory going, even though unemployment in the province is 11 percent. In Prince Edward Island, where the unemployment rate is also 11 percent, it's Russians and Ukrainians who are brought in to work in the fish plants.

The distorting, debilitating effect of equalization "harms productivity everywhere," MacKinnon states. But Ontario, as the largest economy, suffers most. "It could cut us off from what could otherwise be a very bright future," he warns.[7]

The Atlantic Canadian Reality Distortion Field is about to come up against the Ontario Reality Check. Ontario middle-class suburban voters are worried about their own jobs. Many of them are immigrants, still pushing to get the second foot firmly planted. The idea that only 40 percent of all unemployed Ontario workers in the last recession qualified for EI, even though the province had the fourth-highest unemployment rate in the country, while 90 percent of the unemployed in Newfoundland and Labrador received a cheque, is intolerable. The Ontario premier may finally be getting an army.

The Conservatives know this. It is why they stripped the equalization component out of the health transfers that Jim Flaherty announced in December 2011. It is why in the 2012 budget they finally decided to start reining in Maritimers' unemployment entitlements.

The Conservatives will be sorry, some warn. They will be shut out of Atlantic Canada for a generation. What Atlantic Canadians don't get—and won't get, until they finally start to dismantle that damned distortion field—is that no political party will ever form a government without Ontario suburban middle-class voters, and those voters are hurting. They're scared they might lose their jobs, or their mortgages might sink underwater, or their children might still be living at home at 30.

As we mentioned in the previous chapter, some Laurentian elites believe that these frightened voters will make common cause with Quebecers—and, who knows, with Atlantic Canadians, for what it's worth—and bring a progressive party to power. They'll join with the other have-nots grappling with declining industries and populations in exodus to demand more from Ottawa.

But Ontario still gives, whether it wants to or not. It is still the economic engine of the country, even if it's not firing on all cylinders. Policies that retard growth are policies that damage Ontario. The political parties that promise this social program and commit to protect that sacred cow will win votes in the receiving provinces; the political party that promises to protect jobs and keep taxes low will get votes in Ontario. Ontario's natural political allies are now their former colonies in the West, where there is growth and wealth and increasing impatience with those who take rather than give and call it the Canadian way.

Something else is happening, too. As immigrants transform Toronto—and, to a lesser but still real extent, Ottawa and London and other Ontario cities—Asian immigrants are causing the province to look west even more. In the eyes of these new arrivals from Colombo and Manila and Shanghai and Mumbai, the Pacific (or the Indian), not the Atlantic, is their ocean. Their cousins live in Calgary and Vancouver, not Montreal and Halifax. They are turning Ontario from a European, Atlantic province into an Asian, Pacific province. This is another reason the bonds are strengthening between Ontario and the West, at the expense of the East.

And so the Ottawa River Curtain descends, separating the impoverished, dependent Atlantic East from the growing, independent Pacific West. East of the curtain is dependence—demographic decline, aversion to immigrants, provincial budgets addicted to federal handouts. West is aspiration—growing in population, struggling to find its feet in the twenty-first-century economy, bolstered by natural resources in the West and manufacturing (what's left of it) and financial services in Ontario. In the Pacific West there is a rising impatience with the dependency of the

Atlantic East. The Laurentian appeasements are breaking down. Something else is needed.

What is needed, of course, is to lift the curtain. But how? Who will tear down this new wall? No one east of the Ottawa River Curtain seems to have an answer. All they can do is gaze with envy at the West.

5

The Wests

GETTING USED TO BEING IN CHARGE

What is the capital of Western Canada? Is it Vancouver, the country's third-largest city and sole Pacific metropolis? Or is it Calgary, where the wealth of the oil sands is expressed in smart new office towers and endlessly—and we do mean endlessly—sprawling suburbs? And what would Edmonton have to say about either choice?

In fact, none of them qualifies. The capital of Western Canada, the seat of its power and influence, is Ottawa. Nothing expresses the dominance of the West in Confederation like Ottawa today. The national capital is run, lock stock and barrel, by Westerners. The prime minister is from Alberta. Almost half of the governing caucus is from the Prairie provinces, British Columbia, or the territories. Half of the Commons committee chairs are from the West. The governor of the Bank of Canada, the chief justice of the Supreme Court, and the clerk of the Privy Council are all from the West. The West dominates the power centres of the federal government today the way Quebec did under Pierre Trudeau.

Canada evolved profoundly under Trudeau's Quebec influence. Social programs expanded, and the state along with it. The British connection was all but entirely severed. Bilingualism, the Constitution, asymmetrical federalism— if you don't know what that is, don't worry; it died with the Charlottetown Accord—all dominated a capital obsessed over Quebec questions and dedicated to accommodating, even if they could never be satisfied, Quebec's demands.

So it should come as not the slightest shock to anyone to discover that today's Ottawa is increasingly a city of Western values and Western priorities, dominated by Western politicians who lead the first truly Western government in this country's history. Oddly, some Laurentianists seem to resent the new reality. But of course the shoe is no longer on their foot.

"The West wants in," Preston Manning declared as he launched the Reform Party two and a half decades ago. Today the West is so in that other parts of the country are feeling crowded out. Nothing fuels the frustrated impotence of the Laurentian elites like the knowledge that the chairs they once occupied are taken by guys wearing cowboy boots. The West has power because the West has money and growth. In 1985, Manitoba, Saskatchewan, Alberta, and British Columbia collectively accounted for 32 percent of Canada's gross domestic product. In 2010, the figure was 36 percent. In 1985, the population of Calgary was 625,143;

today, it's 1,096,833. Alberta's population is growing at twice the national average; Saskatchewan's population, after years of decline, grew by 6.7 percent between 2006 and 2011. In those same years, Manitoba's rate of population growth, at 5.9 percent, was double what it was in the first half of the decade. As we've observed, the population of the four Western provinces now exceeds the population east of the Ottawa River Curtain.

You might think Ontario would resent the new wealth and influence of the West. There is little sign that Ontario voters do. Protestant Ontario, after all, is rooted in the work ethic. Ontario respects success. There was a time when the impudent colonies to the west needed to be kept in their places. But that time has passed, and Ontario knows it. We are witnessing a new partnership between the old Centre and the new, forged in common interest and by the immigrants who flood into, and bind together, both places.

Here's a funny thing. In the United States, Republicans confidently expected to govern pretty much interrupted throughout the twenty-first century. After all, the southern states had voted GOP ever since the Democratic Party betrayed Jim Crow by bringing in the civil rights acts of the 1960s. And the South was growing, with millions of people moving out of the Rust Belt in search of jobs or retirement sun. As the South grew, the power of the Republican Party would grow with it, strategists figured, making it the natural governing party of the United States.

But it didn't turn out that way. Hispanic immigration

was part of the reason, but internal migration had a lot to do with it as well. All those northern Democrats moving south brought their politics with them, painting bedrock states like Virginia, North Carolina, New Mexico, and Nevada blue. (In the U.S., blue is the colour of the liberal Democrats and red the colour of the conservative Republicans, while in Canada red equals left and blue equals right. The Americans, of course, have it wrong.)

But in Calgary, waves of immigration have had little impact on politics, at least at the federal level. Apart from Redmonton, as it gets called, which occasionally elects a Liberal or even—gasp!—a New Democrat, the province is wall-to-wall Conservative. Upon arriving in Alberta, people seem to shed their political pasts, jam a Stetson on, and head to the polling booth to vote for the nearest Tory. Why is that?

The power of the province's political culture may have something to do with it. A land boom lasting about 20 years and ending with the First World War brought 600,000 Americans into Alberta, which is why the place looks, feels, and sounds more like a state than a province. The discovery of oil turned Alberta from poor and Republican to rich and Republican. There are signs of change—Naheed Nenshi becoming mayor of Calgary; Alison Redford's moderate Progressive Conservatives beating back Danielle Smith's hard-edged Wildrose Party—but the fact remains that Alberta remains the most conservative place in Canada and the beating heart of this government.

The West has always been a resource-based economy, thriving or suffering depending on the price of wheat or potash or softwood or oil. But with the emerging Pacific economies on a lengthy, sustained upward trend, the long-term prospects for those resources are more than encouraging.

Even Manitoba is thriving. The traditional poor cousin of the Prairies now has one of the lowest unemployment rates in the country. There's a bit of oil in the southwest, there's plenty of hydro in the north, agriculture is on the upswing, and a reasonably solid manufacturing sector is holding its own. Manitoba is also more successful than any other province, on a per capita basis, at attracting immigrants under the provincial nomination program, which accounted for over 91 percent of the province's newcomers in 2008 versus Ontario's 2.9 percent. (Most Ontario immigrants arrive under other programs.) In 2010, 15,805 immigrants arrived in Manitoba, the most since the end of the Second World War. Research shows that more than 85 percent of immigrants who arrive in Manitoba stay there. Partly that's because the provincial government obsesses over matching intake to employment shortages. The top three job categories for immigrants in 2009 were industrial butchers, truck drivers, and welders.[1]

Manitoba offers living proof that even those parts of the West that aren't directly affected by the oil sands are prospering. Saskatchewan has oil but is also doing well thanks to high potash and grain prices. The province has reversed years of population decline and is growing again, robustly.

In that same period, Alberta's population increased by 10.8 percent and British Columbia's by 7 percent. So throughout the West, robust growth is a constant. With growth comes wealth. And with wealth comes power.

––––––––

We should really talk about the Wests rather than the West. After all, each province is very different from the others, politically as well as economically. To the east, Saskatchewan used to share with Manitoba a sense that it was in the midst of a long period of decline, alternating between Conservative and NDP governments as they struggled to stem the erosion of population and. Although both provinces are doing better, Saskatchewan is doing *much* better thanks to its own oil reserves, which may be why Saskatchewan (read: conservative) Party Premier Brad Wall is the most popular first minister in the country. Saskatchewan's gaze is turning away from Manitoba toward Alberta.

The mountains that separate B.C. from Alberta are more than a geographical barrier. They separate the Pacific mindset from the Prairie mindset. British Columbia, with an economy historically rooted in lumber and minerals, has a strong labour movement. Alberta, historically a province of farmers, doesn't. British Columbia and Alberta both had long spells of Social Credit government—a once-wacky populist movement that morphed into mainstream conservatism. But British Columbia has also had NDP governments, and pretty radical ones at that, while Albertans are mostly divided between conservatives and *really, really* conservatives. Although both Vancouver and Calgary are rapidly growing, cosmopolitan cities, their federal politics couldn't be further apart.

In Vancouver in the last federal election, 13 Conservatives, seven NDPers, and two Liberals were elected MPs in the Lower Mainland. Despite that third-place finish, Vancouver is one of the few places west of Ontario where Liberals can still be observed in their native habitat. One way to think of Vancouver is as a western outpost for the Laurentian Consensus: a multicultural, politically complex urban recreation of Toronto, with the Pacific Ocean substituting for Lake Ontario.

In Calgary, meanwhile, the population is both culturally and politically more homogeneous, and at the last election the MPs Calgary sent to Ottawa numbered zero NDPers, zero Liberals, and eight Conservatives.

Of course, as we mentioned, even Alberta evolves: Nenshi is socially progressive and a Muslim; Stephen Mandel, mayor of Edmonton, is Jewish. The trouncing that Redford's PCs inflicted on Smith's Wildrose cleaved more or less along an urban/rural divide. And this reveals yet another fracture, not only in the West but across Canada. The white, rural parts of the country, the last places where the descendants of the original settlers can still be found, are deeply more conservative than their multicultural urban counterparts. And when we say white, we mean white. A Statistics Canada survey predicts that by 2031, 60 percent of Vancouver's population will be overseas-born, second only to Toronto's. But in Kelowna the rate will be only 10 percent.

The B.C. interior, the farms of Saskatchewan, the dairy operations in Quebec, and the outports of Newfoundland all hold much in common. They are tied to the land and to the settler culture. They resent and do not comprehend cities, with their multicultures, their gay villages, their exotic foods, and their liberal ways.

While we talk about regions and immigrants and languages, the greatest of divides might be between the country, wherever it is, and the nearest city. The countryside everywhere is in decline, unless it can grow Pinot Noir grapes. Its population is thinning, its economy is fragile, and its mindset is far, far removed from the burgeoning, entrepreneurial, multicultural cauldrons of the cities. But this chasm is universal, to be found as much in the United States and France and Australia as in Canada.

So, yes, there are several Wests: the Wests that divide politically between Prairie and Pacific, between social democrat and conservative, between relative decline and wildfire growth, between immigrant and settler and Aboriginal cultures, between rural and urban, between richer and poorer.

And yet those Wests do have things in common. Politically, they are more inclined to gravitate toward conservative values than their Central and Eastern Canadian counterparts. And those who are not conservative tend to be on the left, leaving centrist liberals in the lurch. We see it in the conservative/social democratic split in Manitoba, Saskatchewan, and British Columbia. We see it as well in the values of the place.

The West, unlike the Maritimes, has never experienced a protracted period of economic decline leading to a sense of defeat and entitlement. The dust bowl, the Depression, and the erosion of the family farm left Westerners frustrated and aggrieved (and dangerously complacent about receiving agricultural subsidies). But they never turned Westerners into a defeated people. Defeat isn't in their bones. However, they have led to what could be called the Western Way, which—after six years of Western-based Conservative government—is increasingly becoming the Canadian Way.

The traumas of the dust bowl and the Depression made Westerners suspicious of banks and debt, which might have saved the country in the 1990s. It was NDP Premier Roy Romanow who first tackled a provincial deficit, followed by Ralph Klein in Alberta. The Reform Party came to Ottawa demanding an end to deficit and debt, which gave Paul Martin the political cover he needed to slash public spending and balance the books. The West, not the East, led the push for fiscal responsibility that has become ingrained within Canadians, at least at the federal level. No federal political party would release an election platform that doesn't at least promise to keep the budget balanced.

Balanced budgets were never a first priority for the Laurentian Consensus, who hewed to Keynesian economics long after the theory had self-evidently failed, once governments got into the habit of running deficits in good times *and* bad. One of the major Keynesian economists of the last half of the twentieth century, John Kenneth Galbraith, hailed from Southwestern Ontario and was much beloved by the Laurentianists. Besides, deficits were necessary to finance the pan-national programs—health care, welfare, housing subsidies, and later child care—by which Central Canadian elites hoped to cobble the nation together through shared values.

Westerners are, by and large, uninterested in such nation-building schemes, and certainly uninterested in subsidizing them. No wonder one of Stephen Harper's first priorities, once he came to power, was to scrap the planned national child care program, instituting instead direct payments to parents.

But that was only the beginning, of course. Cutting the GST, cutting corporate taxes, cutting regulations, loosening environmental constraints, cutting government spending once the recession was over—all of the big-ticket fiscal items of the Harper government have been rooted in the Western aversion to big government and high debt. Some of these ideas the Laurentian elites had reluctantly embraced in the 1990s; the Harper Tories seized them with enthusiasm.

But it's not just about balanced books. It's also about

the family. The West remains, perhaps because of its rural and American roots, a more socially conservative part of Canada. Ralph Klein, as Alberta premier, actively fought against the legalization of gay marriage. In an Ipsos Reid poll that asked whether respondents agreed with the statement that abortion "should not be permitted under any circumstances, except when the life of the mother is in danger," nationally only 13 percent of Canadians said yes. In Alberta, however, the figure was 17 percent, while in Quebec it was only 8 percent. (Interestingly, 16 percent of Ontarians agreed with the statement.)

Back in 2003, when he was leader of the Canadian Alliance, Stephen Harper gave what is now famously known as the Civitas speech, named after the private conservative club in Toronto where he delivered it. Liberals, Harper said, had already followed Margaret Thatcher's and Ronald Reagan's lead in converting from liberal to conservative orthodoxy—although, he added "we do need deeper and broader tax cuts, further reductions in debt, further deregulation and privatization."

But the real challenge lay in confronting "the social agenda of the modern left." Conservatives, he said, must fight for "issues involving the family . . . such as banning child pornography, raising the age of sexual consent, providing choice in education, and strengthening the institution of marriage." Conservatives would have to go slow, he warned. "Rebalancing the conservative agenda will require careful political judgment . . . issues must be chosen carefully . . .

real gains are inevitably incremental." Patience, my friends, patience.

In power, Harper raised the age of sexual consent, cracked down hard on sex offenders, and introduced a bill that would expand police powers to monitor the Web in search of child pornographers. His most important family-values promise will permit income splitting between parents, once the deficit is eliminated, making it possible in more families for one parent to stay home with young children.

Part of the prime minister's learning curve, however, was realizing that, on issues such as capital punishment, abortion, and gay rights, the national debate was settled and Conservatives would reopen it at their political peril. Harper took only a token and half-hearted stab at reopening the gay marriage debate, happily abandoning the idea when part of his own Cabinet voted against it. He has become visibly and publicly impatient with Tory backbenchers who try to drag the abortion debate back into Parliament. "As long as I am prime minister, we are not opening the abortion debate," he declared during the 2011 election campaign. "The government will not bring forward any such legislation, and any such legislation that is brought forward will be defeated as long as I am prime minister."

Even in the West, attitudes are changing in favour of social tolerance. Although Ralph Klein fought the gay marriage legislation, vowing to use the notwithstanding clause to nullify it in his province—Klein had, as it turned out, an uncertain grasp of how the clause and the Constitution worked—Albertans today are broadly supportive of gay marriage. Wildrose Leader Danielle Smith came a cropper in the 2011 Alberta election in part because of homophobic comments by some of her candidates. It turned out that Albertans are no less intolerant toward intolerance than anyone else.

And getting tough on crime may mean limiting parole, but it emphatically does not mean reintroducing capital punishment. Even if most Canadians do support the idea, few want to go through the agony of the public furor that would accompany bringing it back.

Westerners, in short, want their federal government to do less nation building and more family protecting. The differences between them and their Laurentian counterparts are not profound: even a politically polarized Canada remains more consensual by nature than most other countries. But these differences are real and they do matter, because Western values infuse the national government. In that sense, we are all Westerners now.

It comes down to this, the very essence of what we have been trying to say: Westerners are not interlopers who have temporarily seized power, but who will lose it when Ontario voters come to their senses and abandon their crazy flirtation with populist rednecks. Ontario voters—that is, suburban middle-class voters, many of them immigrants—identify more closely with Western values than with those on the other side of the Ottawa River Curtain, because they share the values of success through independence and hard work that are the hallmarks of the pioneer Western spirit, and that are reflected in the latest pioneers from China and India and the Philippines. *This shift is permanent.* Another party may come to power, but no one will ever again be able to govern this country without accounting for the West. There is too much of it, there are too many of them, and they have too much money to be pushed aside. There is an axiom in politics: power follows wealth. The West now has both. Suburban middle-class Ontario voters understand this. Anyone who doesn't will be on the outside, looking in. Forever.

The Big Shift is, in the end, good for Canada. No, it's *great* for Canada. It means that the expanding centres of growth will determine the national agenda, not the brackish backwaters of decline. Instead of wrestling over the last few crumbs of the last piece of the shrunken pie, government will seek to grow the pie. That is the West's gift to Canada: to make it a country of the future, based on policies and principles that look to that future with confidence. We need only look across the Atlantic to see how we would do if led by the alternative.

The challenge for Westerners will be to grow into the leadership they have assumed. The chip has to come off the shoulder once and for all. The West is going to have to become the new Ontario. In exchange for policies that protect its wealth and promote its growth, the West will increasingly need to step up to the plate of national interest. As post-industrial Ontario turns into a region, the Prairies and B.C. will need to stop being one. Now that the West is the new Centre, it will need to start acting like one.

This doesn't mean—it emphatically doesn't mean—new transfer programs that funnel Western wealth into Eastern pockets. Westerners have never been keen on horizontal (region-to-region) transfers, rightly seeing them as a crutch that less prosperous governments use to avoid facing up to their own responsibilities. Leadership doesn't mean just writing a cheque. Leadership means having a coherent idea of where the country ought to go and leading it there. Rather like the Laurentian elites used to do.

We already see signs that the West is ready to assume this role. We see it in Alberta Premier Alison Redford's proposal for a national energy strategy, in Saskatchewan Premier Brad Wall's willingness to speak out on national issues. We could see it elsewhere. British Columbia, Alberta, and Saskatchewan have created a true internal common market, dismantling interprovincial barriers to trade and investment. Manitoba Premier Greg Selinger has committed his province to the project. The next step should be to invite Ontario to join. West of the Ottawa River Curtain, Canada could enjoy a national economic union, with people and goods free to move back and forth without restrictions on certification or the non-tariff barrier local preference. Provinces east of the curtain could be invited to become part of the pact. But as yet there is no sign that anyone there is interested in breaking the old bonds.

The West could also help to forge a stronger union by abandoning its provincial—in the worst sense of the word—obsession with keeping control over economic regulation. Alberta successfully fought the Harper government's efforts to establish a national securities regulator, beating them at the Supreme Court by arguing that the Constitution doesn't give Ottawa such powers. Ted Morton, a thoughtful if sometimes doctrinaire conservative who was Alberta's finance minister at the time of the proposal, warned that if Ottawa were allowed to replace 13 provincial securities regulators with one national one— even though the Harper government proposal was strictly voluntary—Ottawa would soon be coming after "other areas of provincial jurisdiction governing finance, such as insurance, pensions, and financial institutions."[2] Imagine!

Yes, the Harper Conservatives have shown that the federation works better if Ottawa keeps out of the provinces' hair in health care and other areas of social policy. But the provinces, led by the West, could return the favour. It profits everyone, in every sense of the word, if the federal government has the tools and the mandate to promote the economic union. That would involve uploading responsibility for regulating the economy—including insurance, Mr. Morton—creating nationwide standards for professional certification (if you can teach or practise law in Nova Scotia, why not in Manitoba?), and forcing provinces to drop non-tariff barriers that impede the free flow of both labour and capital.

Strong provinces, sovereign within their spheres, encompassed by a strong economic union watched over by the federal government, would make for a stronger country. Ontario has long championed the cause. When will the West take it up?

Asking the West to be the new Centre does not mean asking it to subsidize or prop up, to drain its wealth into sinkholes that never offer so much as a thank you, let alone a return on investment. But the West can lead by exporting its values eastward. Right now those values are conservative, expressed nationally through Stephen Harper.

But you'll remember that there is another side to Western populism: the socially progressive side that gave rise to the CCF and the NDP, to Tommy Douglas and medicare. Social democracy is Western in its messianic zeal, in its conviction that growth and prosperity are around the corner for all. Its proposed solutions are radically different from those of its conservative counterpart, but its ethos, its political impulse, is the same.

And Adrian Dix, the fluently bilingual leader of the British Columbia NDP, could be premier by the time you read this.

6

They Don't Get It
AND WHY THEY DON'T

As we've shown, for many decades Canada was governed by a collection of elites in cities along the St. Lawrence watershed, operating mostly by consensus and implementing that consensus through the government of the day, which at the federal level was more often than not Liberal. Their power began to ebb as immigrants from Asian lands flooded into Canada, bringing with them more conservative views on the importance of protecting both the economy and the community. Middle-class voters of all kinds living in suburbs around Toronto and other large Ontario cities also began to change their views: they too began to worry more about the economy, after the economic shocks of the Great Recession. And the West, once a marginal bastion of conservative parties, grew in wealth, population, and importance, strengthening the Conservative base. On May 2, 2011, Canada's electoral geography experienced a tectonic shift as immigrant and other middle-class voters in Ontario suburbs joined with voters in the West to elect a majority Conservative government, one with values and priorities very different from those of the Laurentian elites. We believe this Big Shift will endure. Yes, the Conservatives will one day be defeated, either by one of the progressive parties or by a merger of the two—but the fact of the Big Shift is permanent. The rise of the West is permanent. And the schism between Ontario's suburban middle class and its urban elites won't be healed anytime soon.

Simple, really. Self-evident, at least to us. And yet a whole lot of people don't get it. Either they don't understand what has happened, or they don't accept it. Because they don't get it, they misinterpret history, misanalyze the present, and misforecast the future. Some people get paid good money to make these mistakes day after day. Professors stand at the front of classrooms and teach their students bosh. Politicians and their aides put together election-campaign strategies that are bound to fail before they start. Columnists pen articles that try to explain away their unrealized predictions. And as failure piles upon failure, with things never turning out as expected, people start to get desperate. The Harper government, they conclude, isn't just bad, it's illegitimate. It has no right to govern. Voters are deluded and deceived. They need to be educated. The rising power of the West is dangerous. It needs to be contained.

How is it possible for such notions to prevail? It's possible because the people who peddle them, even though they have lost power and influence, still hold the keys to the culture. And they are determined to preserve an alternate reality, their reality, for however long it takes, while they wait for the real reality to come to its senses.

They've already been waiting a long time. But they are, if nothing else, patient.

———————

As the Conservatives approached their first anniversary of majority government, columnist Lawrence Martin argued that Canada under Stephen Harper was closer to being a dictatorship than a democracy.

His evidence? Scientists forbidden to speak in public. Deception in the costing of the F-35 fighter jets. Proof of voter suppression and even electoral fraud in the 2011 campaign, along with financing abuses in 2006. Closure and time allocation routinely imposed on bills. The campaign to convince voters in Liberal MP Irwin Cotler's riding that he was planning to step down. Bureaucrats prohibited from releasing information to the media. Immigration officials masquerading as immigrants at a citizenship ceremony. Undermining of environmental reviews. Opposition MPs prevented from attending an environmental summit. Harper's decision to twice have Parliament prorogued. Money funnelled into Tony Clement's riding for the G8 Summit. Rigid control over departmental communications. Suppression of evidence surrounding the treatment of Afghan detainees. Unauthorized use of patients' private files to discredit government critics. "Technically we might still call [Canada] a democracy," Martin concluded. "In practice it's a democracy in name alone."[1]

Martin's dystopian vision of Canada under the Conservatives more or less fulfilled the prophesy of Heather Mallick, a *Toronto Star* columnist who warned during the 2011 election campaign that under a Harper majority, "Canada would increasingly resemble the U.S.," which to her meant "guns on the street, gated communities, rampant drug use, unlimited anonymous corporate political donations, no government safety standards for food and medicine, classrooms that resemble holding pens more than civilized safe rooms for the young to learn . . . If Harper got his majority, these things would hit us like an avalanche."[2]

The media are not the only source of this hysteria. Stephen Clarkson, the esteemed author and political scientist, described the Harper government in a recent book as a "proto-fascist security state" that "threatens the country's constitutional heritage."[3] There have been many such comments about this government.

Erna Paris painted a picture in the *Walrus* of "a country house whose familiar furniture is being rearranged to suit a new master, a 'living room' in which the historical role of government in caring for its citizens has shrivelled; where citizenship is no longer an unambiguous indicator of rights; where inequality has gained a surer footing; and where only the strongest will breathe the air at the top."[4]

There is merit in some of this criticism. The control-freakishness of the Harper government is, indeed, its greatest failing. But is the government truly a threat to democratic freedoms in Canada? Do people really believe it rigged the 2011 election, keeping Jack Layton from becoming prime minister? Is it reasonable to argue that, under the Conservatives, Canada has come to more closely resemble Belarus than Britain?

The rest of the world doesn't think so. The *Economist*'s Democracy Index ranked Canada number eight in 2011, ahead of all other G8 and G20 countries. (Great Britain came in at 18, the United States at 19, and France at 29.) The World Press Freedom Index, compiled by Reporters without Borders, ranks Canada number 10 in terms of press freedom, ahead of Great Britain (28), France (38) and the United States (57). Freedom House, an American independent watchdog organization, publishes an annual report card on the degree of freedom of each nation. Canada always gets the highest possible score, along with the other advanced democracies.

The democracy, it would seem, endures. But the Harper government's most strident critics illustrate a quality within Canadian media and the broader public. The Laurentian elites believe that any government outside its ideological or geographical frame of reference is not a legitimate government. Its policies are not simply wrong, but destructive. The suburban voters who have detached themselves from their former allies in city centres are deluded. The elections that brought such a government to power had to have been corrupted. The Conservative government is not misguided; it is evil. Stephen Harper is evil.

In this respect, the Central Canadian elites resemble the "birthers" who sought to disqualify Barack Obama as president on the hilarious grounds that his birth certificate was fake, and that he was really a foreigner and probably a Muslim and possibly a terrorist.

The Canadian equivalent believe that the Conservatives came to power only because of their vicious attack ads, financed by their radical supporters. Some blame the Westminster system of electing MPs, which can allow a party with about 40 percent of the vote to form a majority government. (They were less concerned when the same system delivered Liberal majorities.) Allegations that overzealous campaign workers impersonated Elections Canada officials in robocalls that sent voters to non-existent polling stations expanded into allegations that dozens—even hundreds—of ridings across the country might have been compromised, throwing the outcome into doubt.

There is nothing unique about this. The same critics were no less hostile to Mike Harris's Ontario Conservatives in the 1990s and Brian Mulroney's Progressive Conservatives in the 1980s, especially during the free trade debate. Whenever the Central Canadian power elites have found the argument not going their way, they have questioned the legitimacy of the other side. Never mind that Pierre Trudeau actually suspended constitutional liberties by invoking the *War Measures Act,* expropriated property through the National Energy Policy, and almost tore the country apart in his efforts to repatriate the Constitution. That's nothing compared to gutting the mandatory long-form census.

There is, of course, a good reason for the particularly high level of vitriol aimed at Stephen Harper. The Laurentian elites are not used to being out of power—certainly not for this long. The last time one of their own was prime minister was 2005. Already, much of what they built—on fiscal policy, foreign policy, health, justice, federalism—has been dismantled. Every year, as Erna Paris mourned, Canada becomes more unrecognizable to them.

The elites are also deeply frustrated. The Harper Way is so self-evidently wrong in their eyes, it is so demonstrably dangerous to national unity, so harmful to the long-term interests of the economy, so clearly the harbinger of a coming war on women, gays, racial minorities, and religious freedom that the 40 percent of votes it received in the last election is inexplicable. Yet what is to be done? Does salvation lie in finding a saviour for the Liberal Party? Is it time to consider the drastic option of merging the Liberals with the NDP? Could Thomas Mulcair be trusted with power of government? If power can be won, is it time to embrace proportional representation, so that the Conservatives can never have their untrammelled way again?

Most important of all, is there a way to sever the still-tenuous bonds between the Ontario suburban voters and the voters in the West that made the Conservative majority possible?

Frustration is an unhealthy emotion: it prevents clear-eyed analysis. If the Laurentian elites were able to give their collective heads a shake, they would realize that all these questions are based on false premises. Garbage in, garbage out, as they say.

Who says 60 percent of voters oppose the Conservatives? If progressives were to unite their forces, some portion of the electorate that doesn't vote Conservative now would start to. We call these people John Manley Liberals, after the former industry, foreign affairs, and finance minister in the Chrétien governments. Manley advocated free trade, investing in research, strong defence, closer security ties to the United States, balanced budgets, and lower taxes. He joined the Liberal Party because that was the party you joined to Get Things Done. After leaving politics, he went on to head the Canadian Council of Chief Executives. Like all Canadians, Manley casts a secret ballot, but it's tempting to wonder whether he voted Liberal or Conservative in 2011. And if it came down to a straight choice between, say, Stephen Harper and Thomas Mulcair, who doubts where Manley's vote would go?

There are millions of voters like John Manley. The knuckle-draggers in the Conservative Party alarm them. They want nothing to do with banning abortion or gay marriage or restoring the death penalty. But it is now abundantly clear to anyone not crazed with rage that Stephen Harper wants nothing to do with any of this either. We believe that, given a choice between the unpleasantness of Stephen Harper and what they would see as the irresponsibility of any government that had NDP in its DNA, they would gravitate to the Tories.

There are some within the Laurentian elites who have glimpsed one vital truth: the path to power for any party lies in winning over the Ontario suburban middle class, both settler culture and immigrant. In a remarkable political coincidence, both Liberal and NDP strategists are advocating the same strategy: reforge the alliance between Ontario and Quebec.

John Duffy caused a stir in Liberal circles with a 2012 article called "Discipline of Powerlessness." Now that the once-dominant party had become used to being in opposition, the former advisor to Paul Martin argued, it needed to plot a long-term strategy back to power.

"A 'Two Canadas' pattern may be emerging," Duffy writes. The Conservatives are abandoning the middle class, he argued, in favour of tax cuts that benefit the better-off most. Even more important—politically, the country is bifurcating into an affluent West whose economy is based on resource extraction, and a struggling East tied to manufacturing. Liberals, he believes, "can convincingly tag the Conservatives as favouring the commodity economies of their political heartland at the expense of the rest."

As for the purported electoral alliance between Ontario and the West, "Ontario seems a less-promising alliance partner for the Tory West, and perhaps a more plausible one for post-industrial Quebec and Atlantic Canada."[5]

In essence, Duffy proposes a return to the past: a Quebec-based Liberal Party facing a Western-based Conservative Party, with Ontario the prize and victory assured by protecting that province's industry at the expense of Western resources.

Inconveniently, for this line of reasoning, Quebecers appear unwilling to co-operate. Their impetuous fling with Jack Layton's NDP has settled into a comfortable marriage under Thomas Mulcair. In the next election, the Bloc Québécois may or may not rise from the dead; the Conservatives may or may not improve their standing in Quebec. But a wholesale abandonment of the Official Opposition for the third party among French Quebecers? Why would they do such a thing?

Strangely enough, Duffy's strategy could work, but for the NDP rather than the Liberals. This may have been what Thomas Mulcair was thinking when he accused Stephen Harper of infecting Canada with Dutch disease.

The NDP chose well in picking the former Cabinet minister from Jean Charest's Liberal government to replace Jack Layton. Not only did Mulcair's victory cement NDP gains in Quebec; his tough, savvy approach to confronting the Conservatives was a breath of refreshing realpolitik from a party historically prone to dreaming of the New

Jerusalem when it needed instead to grub for votes. Mulcair had barely settled into Stornoway when he repeated, loudly, a core campaign theme: rapacious development and exports of oil and other natural resources, without concern for the environmental cost, were pushing up the value of the Canadian dollar, rendering manufacturing industries in Ontario and Quebec uncompetitive and damaging their economies. The Netherlands suffered from similar affliction in the 1960s, hence the Dutch diagnosis.

Postmedia Network columnist Michael Den Tandt was the first to spot the political consequences. "It's all about Ontario," he wrote, soon after Mulcair repeated his claims in a CBC interview. "Mulcair is making a play, which we can expect him to broaden and deepen in the years ahead, to destroy the May 2, 2011, political coalition between Alberta and Ontario, which excludes Quebec. In effect, the NDP is writing off the Prairies and staking its future hopes of forming a government on Ontario."[6]

As a political strategy, reforging the Ontario/Quebec axis makes far more sense for the NDP than for the Liberals. They are the party with 57 seats in the province already. They are the party with a Quebec leader. If it really is the 1970s all over again, with a progressive Quebec-based party and a conservative Western-based party fighting it out for Ontario, the NDP is now the natural candidate to seize the role once played by the Liberals, making Thomas Mulcair the natural heir to Pierre Trudeau.

There is, of course, that other Trudeau. As this book went

to press, Pierre's eldest son, Justin, appeared pretty much certain to win the Liberal leadership in April 2013. The younger Trudeau has inherited his father's charisma and his mother's hair. Whatever his other talents—and they remain to be determined, much less proven—the young Quebec MP has stirred at least an echo of the mania that surrounded his father's rise to the prime ministership 45 years ago.

That mania eventually faded, and Justin's will too. The question—and it will take years to answer—is whether he is also heir to the talent and the tenacity of his father. While we wait to find out, and while the Liberal Party continues its efforts to rebuild and rebrand, Thomas Mulcair remains the most credible and dangerous opponent facing Stephen Harper, a situation that is not likely to change in time for the next election.

Let's assume that Quebec stays solidly NDP right up until that election. That's not a given—the Bloc Québécois could surge back to life; the Liberals under Trudeau could recover ground; the Conservatives are not prepared to surrender the field—but let's assume Mulcair succeeds in securing his hold on the province.

Let's assume, as well, that the NDP doesn't back away from its stand that oil sands development is damaging not only the environment but also the Canadian economy, and that the solution is to force the oil companies to pay more in environmental compensation. Now let's pretend it is October 2015 and we're in the middle of the next federal election. How is the NDP strategy playing out?

As expected, the West has turned into a wasteland. A party born of Prairie populism is now as toxic as the Liberals were after the NEP. The party will hold a few seats in Vancouver, and maybe one in Winnipeg, but otherwise it's a shutout.

The strategy is also failing in Ontario. There are several reasons for this. As we suggested previously, immigrant suburban voters simply don't see themselves reflected in the Quebec mirror. These immigrants are Pacific oriented, English speaking, and economically and socially more conservative than Quebecers. They don't get Quebec's obsession with culture and language. They don't get the corporatist approach to managing the economy. They do get that Quebec's model is sustained only by transfers from the rest of the country, and to the extent Ontario might emulate that model it would spell disaster. Why should they vote with Quebecers? What have Quebecers ever done for them?

The broader Ontario population, at least outside the downtowns, shares the same view. They don't see how it helps the Ontario economy to damage the Alberta economy. In politics as in business as in life, it's never a good idea to punish success. A raft of economists (not to mention Bank of Canada Governor Mark Carney) have dumped all over Mulcair's Dutch disease theory. Manufacturing, they point out, is in decline through much of the developed world, in countries without oil as much as in countries with oil, in Michigan as much as in Ontario. Of course polluters should pay, but shutting down the oil sands and cancelling the pipelines makes no sense as a growth strategy for the Canadian economy.

Beyond that, Ontario voters recognize that the NDP's efforts to divide the country between West and Rest is bad for everyone. Critics complain that the Conservatives are divisive, and that their policies and attitudes have alienated Quebec voters. But at least the Conservatives have tried to keep Quebec in the tent by recognizing the Quebec people as a nation, granting Quebec a seat at UNESCO, fixing the so-called fiscal disequilibrium, harmonizing the sales tax with compensation, promising a new bridge for Montreal, and generally keeping out of the province's hair.

What is the NDP offering in exchange? Paying yet greater attention to Quebec, even as the party willfully alienates the Western provinces. How does that help things?

For millions of Ontario voters, the whole notion simply confirms what everyone already expected: the NDP still isn't ready to be trusted with government. The Conservatives are getting long in the tooth; Stephen Harper's secretive, autocratic, and increasingly scandal-plagued regime is anything but popular. But the books are balanced, unemployment is manageable, and growth continues to outpace the U.S. and Europe. With a heavy heart, suburban Ontario delivers the Conservatives another majority.

If you are truly convinced that it is the Liberals who will confront the Tories in 2015, then simply swap "NDP" and "Mulcair" in the above scenario with "Liberal" and "Trudeau." Nothing much changes.

Of course, it doesn't have to play out this way. Politics is like the stock market—accurate predictions are hard to make. One scandal too many for the Conservatives, one counterintuitive policy proposal from the NDP, a great Liberal revival under Justin—a huge foot-in-mouth on debate night, and everything could change. Events, dear boy, events. But all else being equal, we do not believe a Quebec-based NDP or Liberal Party can capture a large swath of Ontario seats with a strategy aimed at decoupling Ontario and Western voters—especially through a policy that seeks to punish the West. Such a policy would be bad for the national economy and bad for national unity. It's hard to see how it would sell in Mississauga.

If the Conservatives are re-elected next time out, the Laurentian elites will be beside themselves. A few might ask themselves some tough questions about how disconnected they've become from the mainstream, but most will simply blame the mainstream.

The Laurentian elites make a very large sound. They are heavily represented in the media: they dominate the national press gallery, they speak through the *Toronto Star* and the *Ottawa Citizen* and the Montreal *Gazette* and the *Globe and Mail.* (Though John Ibbitson is not simply waving the company flag when he points out that the *Globe* is making heroic efforts to broaden its reach both in Ontario suburbs and in the West, where its Vancouver bureau now rivals its Ottawa counterpart in size.) They are a common sight in universities—though in the humanities and various -*ology* departments more than in the sciences or commerce streams. They write plays and publish books and paint Stephen Harper in the nude. Their voice today is as powerful as it ever was, except that they no longer control the political agenda and are unlikely to control it ever again. With every new arrival from Mumbai, with every moving van trundling west, with every dollar generated by the emerging economies of Alberta and Saskatchewan, with every new seat that gets added to the House of Commons, they wane. This goes in only one direction, and not in their favour.

They simply don't get that the country has moved on.

7

The Conservative Century

WHY THE TORIES WILL RULE, AND HOW
THEY'LL BE DEFEATED

Shifts as enormous as the ones we've been talking about—shifts in where people live, where they come from, what they value—are bound to upset a whole orchard's-worth of political apple carts. If any more proof were needed of the seismic forces reshaping Canada, our national politics would provide it. Less than a decade ago, the Liberal Party was a monolith, racking up majority government after majority government, seemingly destined—just as Margaret Thatcher thought she was destined—to go on and on. The conservative movement was fragmented into two rump parties: one of them was flirting with bankruptcy, the other kept changing its name; neither was ever going to taste power. And the NDP had become so marginal that its greatest challenge seemed to be retaining party status in the House of Commons. We don't need to tell you that things have changed.

Something fundamental is happening. Politics in Canada is dividing along ideological lines, and those divisions will only grow sharper over time. As we showed in the previous chapter, we believe that fortune favours the Harper government in the next election. But we don't believe this is about the next election. We believe it is about the next decade, the next generation, and beyond. We believe that the Conservative Party will be to the twenty-first century what the Liberal Party was to the twentieth: the perpetually dominant party, the natural governing party. Again, we don't say that this is a good thing or a bad thing. We simply say that it's a thing. The root of the Laurentian elites' frustration is their inability, or refusal, to accept this truth.

Such a claim will no doubt offend partisans of the other parties and progressives in general. But to deny it is to deny causality. We might call such denial the Anything Can Happen school of political analysis. Making political predictions is foolish and rash because—Anything Can Happen! Don't count the Liberals out because—Anything Can Happen! Don't expect that the economy will always be the most important issue because—well, you get it. The Anything Can Happen list is endless and includes asteroids.

We've both spent uncomfortable mornings trying to explain why the electoral night before didn't go quite as we'd predicted. But we cling to causality nonetheless. For example: True, no one predicted the collapse of the Bloc Québécois in the last election, least of all the Bloc itself.

But the strong possibility of a Conservative majority, the bleak fundamentals for the Liberals, and the potential for Jack Layton's NDP to make substantial gains were known to pollsters and to strategists in all parties long before the writ was dropped.

Moreover, we believe certain political fundamentals have fallen into place that will ensure Conservative dominance for the foreseeable future. That does not mean Conservatives will govern forever. A new, progressive coalition is forming that will challenge, and from time to time defeat, the Conservatives. We believe Quebec could become a powerful base for that movement. But we think that province holds promise for Conservatives, too.

We hope you didn't just throw this book (or Kindle, or Kobo, or whatever) across the room. No, we are not jettisoning our own thesis. But there are some things about Quebec politics that rarely get considered, because the narrative of that province is entirely controlled by Laurentian media and Laurentian politicians. So hear us out, but first allow us to set the stage a little.

The New Natural Governing Party

The Conservative Party is not the Stephen Harper Party. Yes, Harper and his closest advisors were the first to anticipate the tremendous political potential of the Big Shift. He recognized that the West was transforming from a region of protest to an emerging centre of power, that Canada was shifting its economic and cultural focus from the Atlantic to the Pacific, leaving the Laurentian Consensus vulnerable. He saw the potential of winning away immigrant voters from the Liberals. He exploited the growing frustration of the suburban middle class in Ontario with a federal agenda that was more interested in expanding entitlements than in giving them a tax break. He saw that crime, whatever the statistics might say, was a lurking concern for many.

He was able to make a bankrupt Progressive Conservative Party believe that a merger with his Canadian Alliance would be a marriage of equals, when it clearly was not. He smothered the evangelicals within his own movement, convincing them that the quarter loaf they would receive from him was more than would ever be offered by anyone with a chance of actually delivering on an election promise. Harper's greatest achievement has been to forge, over four elections, a modern Conservative coalition with the potential to become an enduring force in Canadian politics, one that will long outlast him.

This new coalition enjoys a demographic cohesiveness and diversity—immigrants in coalition with Old Canada; suburban Ontario in coalition with the West—that the Progressive Conservatives of the past never did. They were always about yoking together discontented Westerners with nationalist Quebecers and Ontario voters fed up with the Liberal hegemony. Such a combination was never stable and never likely to last for long, which is why there were so few conservative federal governments in the twentieth century and why they always ended badly.

Though less than a decade old, the new Conservative Party is already sinking deep roots, based on shared values across different regions. Those values are simple, ideologically consistent, and pragmatic. While Harper occasionally throws the old Reform base a bone—scrapping the gun registry and the Wheat Board, putting the *Royal* back in the navy and air force—he concentrates most of his efforts on convincing that broader coalition of support that his government is doing three simple but vital things: minding the till, watching the border, keeping criminals off the streets.

Harper's Conservative Party is emphatically *not* socially conservative. Harper knows that letting Conservatives become identified with fundamentalist Christian values—with opposition to abortion or gay rights, or with a law-and-order agenda that veers into support for the death penalty—would tear the party apart and alienate it from the electoral mainstream. Even socially conservative immigrants would flee a party that became branded as intolerant. They know that a party that limits rights for gays will one day be tempted to limit rights for religious minorities. But Harper works overtime to assure them that nothing like this is or *ever will be* on his agenda. That is why those who fear or long for the sort of culture wars that afflict the United States will never see those fears (or hopes) realized.

But simply because Canadians don't want to reopen the abortion debate or fight over capital punishment does not mean that there are no ideological divides. There are, and Harper has successfully moulded the Conservative Party to fit the shape of one half of that divide. For some, this is not only intolerable, but simply impossible.

According to this syllogism, Canada is a relentlessly centrist, consensus-driven society. The Conservatives have won three elections, gaining more votes each time. Therefore, the Harper government must now be a centrist, consensus-driven government. Michael Den Tandt of Postmedia Network outlined this theory best, about a year into the Harper majority. In the Harper agenda, he maintained, "there is nothing that could arguably not have been introduced by a Liberal Party led by a John Manley (minister of everything during the Chrétien years), or a Frank McKenna (former premier of New Brunswick)—in other words, by conservative Liberals." After more than six years of Conservative government, "when one surveys the grand sweep of federal policy, looking for truly important structural changes or efforts to roll back the sheltering arms of the Canadian state, one finds—nothing. . . . The Harperites, one year into their majority, are not doing anything dramatically different from what a Chretien-style Liberal party might have been expected to do."[1]

We don't buy this, of course. On immigration reform, on pension reform, on employment insurance reform, on tax cuts, on the law-and-order agenda, on Israel, on the environment—*on, on, on*—if this isn't a sharply Conservative government, at least by Canadian standards, then we would like to see one described.

In *The Vertical Mosaic,* John Porter's seminal work on Canadian politics and culture, the Ottawa-based sociologist argues that Canadian political parties brokered various regional, linguistic, and ethnic interests, but that the day would soon come when parties migrated to ideologically distinct terrains that left voters with a clear choice between left and right. Porter called this "Creative Politics." Well, better late than never. Stephen Harper has forged his coalition around a "less is more"—or perhaps "less, not more"—view of the state. This doesn't mean that the Harper Conservatives have attacked the state in its entirety. Public health care, for example, remains intact and well funded. But any notion of expanding the state—through, say, a national daycare or pharmacare program—is anathema to these Conservatives.

Why is this? Heaven knows there are enough public opinion data out there that say that Canadians want a national daycare or pharmacare program. If this truly were a centrist, pragmatic, Manley Liberal government, then surely the Conservatives would at least mouth platitudes in support of such programs, if only to curry favour with voters. The reason is that the polling data are false, and the Conservatives know it. Or, to be more precise, pollsters who report broad popular support for new national social programs fail to burrow far enough into what the respondents are actually thinking. If they did, they'd discover that, while most Canadians want more government-delivered services, they just don't trust government to deliver those services. Pollsters need to ask these questions: (1) "Are you in favour of this or that socially progressive program?" The answer will likely be yes. (2) "Do you trust government to deliver that program efficiently?" The answer will likely be no. (3) "Thinking forward five years, if this program were brought in today, do you think the problem it is designed to address will be better?" Again, the answer will be no.

The Nanos/IRPP poll that we referenced earlier in the book demonstrates exactly this point. Health care was the number-one priority for most voters, but also the issue they had the least confidence government could do anything to improve. In other words, people think that new government programs would be nice, but they don't trust government to deliver those programs. Which leads Tory supporters to conclude that government is the problem, not the solution. Which leads the Harper government to avoid grand new schemes.

The twin shocks of the last decade—September 11 and the financial crisis—have left people wary and even fearful. Globalization, whatever its blessings, has sent the manufacturing sector into a prolonged slump. The rise of China and other emerging economies presents tremendous opportunities, but also threatens the traditional, comfortable assumptions of Western dominance. These themes run through private conversations and public discourse, interweaving and reinforcing each other. These themes will dominate the public agenda—they will be on people's minds—for years and decades to come. The Conservatives get the Big Shift.

They get the concerns of the troubled middle class. This is why they win elections. They will continue to win elections, more often than not, until these fundamentals change.

Here's an argument for why we're wrong. Governments get old. They do something that angers this group, then something that angers that group. They chip away at their own coalition, seemingly unable to help themselves. In the case of the Harper Conservatives, the Tories have already successfully asked for a mandate from the voters three times, and will be asking next time for a fourth. Rare is the political leader who can pull off a hat-trick-plus-one. At the federal level, no one has managed it since Mackenzie King. The Tories' EI reforms will cost them seats in Atlantic Canada. Their bumbling on the costs of the F-35s, the increasing arrogance and chronic secrecy, the unpleasantness in Guelph—these and a thousand cuts will slowly eat away at support in the 905. The Tory majority is not large; the net loss of a dozen or so seats in the next election could drop them into minority government territory. If so, the NDP and the Liberals would be sorely tempted to bring the government down. Big Shift, Big Schmift. Governments defeat themselves all the time. Eventually, this one will too.

We get this argument; we just don't buy it, for three reasons. First—and we know we're becoming tiresome about this—the prospect of an NDP-led minority government propped up by an enfeebled Liberal Party would drive many voters—those Manley Liberals—into the arms

of the Conservatives. Two-party, ideologically divided elec-
torates choose conservative governments more often than
progressive governments. Count U.S. presidents, or British
prime ministers. Or Australian PMs, for that matter.

Second, as we mentioned, 30 seats will be added to the
House of Commons in the next election, mostly in underrepresented suburbs around Toronto, Calgary, Edmonton,
and Vancouver. Preliminary analyses, once the outlines of
the new ridings were released by Elections Canada, suggested the Tories were favoured to take most of them, cush-
ioning their losses elsewhere.

Third, we believe there is a strong possibility of the
Conservatives, over time, making gains in Quebec.

Now this should make no sense at all. You know the
Laurentian narrative: having failed to win over the soft
nationalist vote through four attempts, Stephen Harper
has given up trying. His government's policies are so many
red flags waved in front of Quebecers: honouring the
Queen, cutting back on equalization components in transfers, toughening employment insurance, cutting funding
to Radio-Canada, and on and on and on.

Sooner or later, by this reasoning, the Péquistes will
hold another referendum on separation, one they could win
because Ottawa will be able to put forward no champion to
defend the idea of Canada, because the Conservatives are so
weak in Quebec.

Maybe. But maybe not.

The massive global and demographic trends that we've

talked about have influenced population migrations, social values, language, and economics in Quebec society as much as anywhere else, if only by their conspicuous absence. Political reality dictates that the Big Shift will influence how at least some people vote in Quebec. New questions are being asked: How central should the role of the state be in the economy? Why is there so much corruption? How can Quebecers enjoy a progressive society *and* a solvent government, while bringing down unemployment and avoiding population decline? We saw politicians in all three parties grapple with those questions during the summer 2012 Quebec election. For the PQ, it was an even greater reliance on linguistic protectionism, coupled with obnoxious promises to limit the wearing of religious headgear and other symbols—though a discreet crucifix would be perfectly acceptable, because it represented the province's cultural heritage, don't you know. For the Liberals, it was the promise of massive royalties from Plan Nord, Jean Charest's 25-year blueprint for resource development. For all parties, it was a devout promise to get to the bottom of the corruption and clean it up.

Did you notice what wasn't in any of that? National unity, sovereignty, identity. Quebecers aren't focused on these issues right now. They want jobs, and services, and affordable tuition, and bridges that don't fall on their heads. And if any more proof were needed, the astonishing success of François Legault's newly minted CAQ, with its vaguely right-of-centre agenda, provided it. The CAQ's popular vote was only 5% lower than the PQ's. The Laurentian assumption that Quebec's place within or outside Canada is the only question that matters is increasingly false. Inside Canada or out, Quebecers are no different from anyone else. They want a society that works.

"Many voters are not interested anymore in the debate on the political future of the province," André Pratte, editor of *La Presse*, observed during the campaign. "It's not that people don't have views for or against separation. It's just that they know the thing will not be solved, if it can be solved, in the foreseeable future. Therefore, why not have a government that puts all its energy in attacking more immediate problems, for instance, the indecent delays before getting an appointment with a doctor or care in an emergency ward?"[2]

Up until now, the impatience with the status quo has come from the left, from the Occupy movement and the student protesters who demand that the government pay attention to them, to their needs, to their priorities. The embrace of Jack Layton's NDP in the last election reflected that urgent desire to break the mould, to find a better way, to get past the tired dogmas of the turbulent past, to create a new turbulence.

But there is an alternative, a Conservative alternative, to banging pots and pans.

Whatever else the Harper government might be, it is not corrupt. Quebecers are tired of corruption. The scent of it in the Federal Liberal Party brought out through the sponsorship scandal destroyed what was left of the party in Quebec outside English Montreal. Allegations coming out of the Charbonneau Inquiry into massive corruption in the construction industry, and arrests involving construction magnates and politicians, contaminated the legitimacy of the Charest government. No one seriously believes the Parti Québécois is entirely above suspicion.

But say what you will, no one has yet caught a Conservative politician guiltily grubbing around inside a cookie jar. A pork barrel, yes, especially in Tony Clement's Parry Sound–Muskoka riding. Election shenanigans, quite possibly, in Guelph and elsewhere. But no one has gotten rich by being a too-well-connected Conservative. International Cooperation Minister Bev Oda was told she had no future in Cabinet after being caught upgrading to a luxury hotel and ordering a $16 glass of orange juice. No one has discovered the prime minister encouraging a bank to offer a loan to a friend. The government may be dictatorial, philistine, and anti-democratic, but at least it's clean.

That reputation could sell in Quebec. Imagine a Tory Quebec election narrative something like this: We know you don't like us. Maybe we're insensitive, maybe we're hard-hearted. Maybe we like the Queen too much. But we're honest. We're not in government to make money for ourselves. And we're responsible. We balance our books. We keep taxes low. We clear away the regulatory underbrush so that businesses can grow. We protect core public services, but we encourage the private sector; we encourage open competition rather than quiet deals and government subsidies. It's working in other parts of the country. Why don't you give it a try?

The results of the last election and the student protests are harbingers of a debate to come about the role of the state in society and the direction the province should take. Quebecers are noticing that their province looks a lot like Europe, with its massive debt, high taxes, state-directed industrial policy, high unemployment, and growing civil unrest. The Canadian version of the austerity battle must come to Quebec sooner or later. The NDP and/or the Liberals (and that forward slash could mean everything) will hold the banner of the federalist, progressive status quo. But what party will speak for the taxpayer? That party might win far, far fewer seats than the NDP did in 2011, but it could also expand from the present Conservative rump of old Union Nationale *bleus* around Quebec City. A Conservative coalition is waiting to be built in Quebec. It might be a minority of the vote, but it might perform much better than electing the five lonely MPs who represent the Conservatives in the House right now.

Over time, the inevitable erosion of support in other parts of the country could be compensated for by modest but important gains in Quebec. Lose a dozen seats here; gain a dozen seats there. Focus relentlessly on the suburban middle class. Continue to own the economy as an issue, with crime on the side. Protect the immigrant vote through robust immigration. To us, it has a natural governing feel.

The Liberal Party and the Black Knight

Of course, as we and many others have noted, the majority of voters are currently outside this Conservative coalition. While every bit as concerned as Conservative supporters about how things are going, they believe that government can and should be part of the solution. But as we all know, progressives are splitting their votes between two parties, just as conservatives did in the 1990s. Jean Chrétien mused that perhaps he should have taken the advice of some of his ministers and invited the NDP into his Cabinet back when it was the social democrats who were at the low ebb. In hindsight, maybe he should have. Because now it is the NDP who is calling the shots. Even half of all Liberal supporters now believe that the NDP has the best chance of stopping Stephen Harper and the Conservatives in the next election.

One of the great mistakes that political observers made in the 1990s was concentrating on the schism within the conservative movement, which caused virtually everyone to miss the rot eating away at the foundations of the Liberal Party. This myopia was entirely a product of the Laurentian elites. Because the Liberal Party was their party, and because the Conservatives were even more than usually in disarray, the only contest for power that mattered seemed to be the contest for the Liberal leadership. The contest has been going on, with ever-increasing bitterness, for a generation: Trudeau versus Turner, Turner versus Chrétien, Chrétien versus Martin. But while the battles raged, the party imperceptibly withered. This had begun as far back as the 1957 election, when voters throughout the West abandoned the Liberal Party for John Diefenbaker. They never returned—Trudeau's National Energy Policy saw to that. French Quebec abandoned the Liberals for Brian Mulroney in 1984, in part thanks to Trudeau's successful patriation of the Constitution in the teeth of French opposition. (When will Liberals, who worship Trudeau like Republicans worship Reagan, accept that their god helped destroy their party?) The Liberal Party today is only slightly less moribund in Quebec outside Montreal than in Saskatchewan outside Regina. By the turn of the millennium, the Liberal Party had begun to resemble the Black Knight in *Monty Python and the Holy Grail,* who challenges King Arthur to a duel. As Arthur hacks off limb after limb, the Black Knight retorts: "It's only a flesh wound."

With the collapse of the Progressive Conservatives following Brian Mulroney's heroic but failed attempt at constitutional reconciliation through the Meech Lake and Charlottetown accords, the identification of the Laurentian elites with the Liberal Party became total. Though they had lost both the West and French Quebec, the Liberals and the Laurentianists consoled themselves with the knowledge that so long as Ontario remained loyal, they would continue to dominate both the government and the governing agenda. And they could always count on the support of new Canadians, a quarter million of whom arrived each year, ready to cast a Liberal ballot as soon as they received citizenship.

But as we've seen, the immigrant vote was another limb

that the Conservatives were about to slice away, using the economy as the sword. Meanwhile, the Liberals were reaching the tragic final act of their political melodrama. Martin versus Chrétien, Dion versus Ignatieff, Ignatieff versus Rae. Today, it's hard to identify the various factions within the Liberal Party. It's also hard to find a pulse.

In recalling the Liberal civil war, it's important to remember this above all: neither side stood for anything. To be sure, one side was a bit more worried about balancing the books, a bit more pro-American, a bit more concerned about the estrangement of the West; the other side was a smidge more socially progressive, anti-American, and Central Canada–centric. But the differences were mostly minor and easily bridgeable. The real fight was simply a fight for power. The Liberal Party believes in being in power. Which means that, after three lost elections and three failed leaders, it believes in nothing at all.

Parties die. The Social Credit Party was once a force in the land. The Progressive Conservatives produced several prime ministers. There are even a few historians who can tell you about the United Farmers and the Anti-Confederates. The Bloc Québécois may not be long for this world.

Liberals appear to hold in Justin Trudeau the possibility of salvation. And Trudeau's advisors do understand the imperative for both their leader and their party to break the Laurentian death grip. John Duffy, in a fall 2012 television panel, predicted that Trudeau would be the first "post-Laurentian leader."

But what Trudeau must also get is that his party is organizationally extinct in large swaths of the country. A few good polls will not cure what ails the Liberal brand. Unless he can rebuild the base of the Liberal Party—reaching out in particular to Asian immigrants, middle-class suburbanites, and voters in the West, the party is destined to wither away, eking out a few seats in its urban bastions, raising just enough money to keep the lights on, praying for a minority government in which it will hold the balance of power. The old guard of the NDP can tell them all about it.

But that old guard is itself irrelevant, having tried and failed to stop Thomas Mulcair from becoming leader. Mulcair is now at the head of NDP 2.0, a confident, energetic, new progressive voice powered by a Quebec contingent that was first elected in a moment of electoral frenzy but that is settling nicely into its role as the voice of progressive Quebec in Ottawa.

The NDP as We've Never Seen It Before

Today's NDP is radically different from the one that emerged from the Co-operative Commonwealth Federation in the early 1960s. NDP 1.0 was a loose coalition of farmers, progressive Christians, and labour unionists. In more recent times, it rolled in left-wing academics, social activists of various stripes, and progressive municipal politicians such as Jack Layton himself.

But NDP 2.0 is a very different beast. It has all but severed its agrarian roots. Canada's farmers left for the Tories a long time ago. The progressive Christian element, while still part of the party's activist class, is marginal. NDP 2.0 voters are mostly an urban, secular lot.

Interestingly, NDP 2.0 is potentially a tighter coalition than the original version. Not only does it have a compelling claim to the social activist set, it is also winning the creative class away from the Liberals. And while NDP 2.0 is decidedly more francophone than NDP 1.0, it would be a mistake to think that these are nationalist voters temporarily slumming with another party. Yes, many NDP voters chose the BQ in the past. But they were attracted more to the Bloc's progressive approach to public policy issues than by a desire to seek an independent Quebec. The truth is that most hardcore separatists stuck by the BQ in the May 2011 election.

If forging a taxpayers' coalition in Quebec represents Harper's opportunity to grow his base, the best hope for the NDP is to build a national anti-austerity movement. There are natural constituencies to be found in Atlantic Canada and in city centres across the country. An effectively performing NDP could push aside the Liberals in Toronto, Montreal, and Vancouver, while also connecting with progressives in Winnipeg, Regina, and Edmonton. In particular, the revival of the provincial NDP in British Columbia under Adrian Dix offers a potentially powerful new base of support for the federal party, complementing the new base in Quebec. From their respective national bases, the NDP and the Conservatives would fight for the support of—say it with us—suburban middle-class voters in Ontario. Mulcair's Dutch disease strategy, which aims to consolidate support among vulnerable manufacturing workers whose jobs have been lost or threatened thanks to a soaring dollar fuelled by oil sands exports, is clearly an opening volley in that campaign.

The Laurentian elites, having grudgingly conceded that the Liberal Party may be a permanently losing bet, are urging the NDP to move to the centre, just as some analysts insist the Conservatives have done. Canada is a consensual society, they reiterate, failing to mention that they embody that consensus. When progressives do come to power, they point out, they get there by adopting conservative orthodoxy. Tony Blair was dubbed "Thatcher's son" because he ended nearly two decades of Labour defeats by embracing the principal tenets of Thatcherism. John F. Kennedy cut taxes; Jimmy Carter launched the war against inflation; Bill Clinton balanced the budget by slashing entitlements.

But while we accept that most Canadians embrace a broad social consensus, a political consensus, even of the left, may not be easily achieved. The new progressive coalition will be driven by opposition to—actually, it comes closer to hatred for—the Conservative autocracy of Stephen Harper. The key to uniting this group will not be a strategy of creeping to the middle. As Harper and the Tories have shown, a harder-edged, more definitive brand works best for the right. It will work best for the left, too.

If the NDP is to defeat the Tories, it will need to take diametrically opposed positions on fundamental issues. Never mind dollars for daycare. Tax the rich, slash military spending, subsidize university tuition, and be done with it. Opposition to the Conservatives, to be successful, will have to be fundamental. Genuinely progressive policies, sold by a genuinely compelling leader, will drive previously uncommitted voters to the polls, countering the partisan activism of the Conservative base.

We accept that there is a contradiction here. To win power, the NDP must galvanize activists across the country behind a genuinely, even emphatically, progressive party powered by a platform that offers a clear alternative to the red-meat Conservatism offered by Stephen Harper. Yet the NDP must also appeal to suburban middle-class voters in Ontario, who are fiscally cautious. Social democratic governments in Europe—and in Saskatchewan and Manitoba, for that matter—have succeeded by convincing voters of their fiscal bona fides. How is an NDP government to mobilize and expand its base without frightening Brampton? How is that circle to be squared?

Not easily, is the answer. The truth is that in countries dominated by polarized two-party systems, or systems where other parties are marginal, conservatives usually win. That is the principal reason Stephen Harper has made destroying the Liberal Party his life's mission. Did you take our advice and check out the performance of conservative parties in two-party systems? Well, here's your answer:

Republicans held the White House for 36 of the 60 years between 1952 and 2012; Conservatives were in 10 Downing Street for 37 years; the Liberal (really Conservative) Party in Australia governed for 38.

That is the most important reason why, in a post-Liberal world, the Conservatives will be the new natural governing party. In two-party systems, conservatives usually win. But it is a contract the NDP is also happy to sign, for the deal gives it at least a reasonable shot at power—something that up until May 2, 2011, no one ever expected to see.

And that may be the most important reason why the Liberals should merge with the NDP, while there is still something left to merge.

Now, people who propose such a merger as though it were no more difficult than making a roux are deluded. Turning two political parties into one is enormously difficult. It took the Conservatives a decade, and that was simply a question of healing a schism within the old Progressive Conservative Party. It wouldn't have happened when it did had the Progressive Conservatives not gone through a dispiriting leadership campaign that left the party bereft of funds. Party elites lose their privileges when parties merge—at least some of them do—and some MPs of long standing know that they will likely win re-election for as long as they choose to run, whatever happens. As long as the fundraising machinery can generate the bare necessities, reasons to avoid a merger will always trump reasons to merge. There is too much history, and pride, at stake.

But at some point, voters and donors are likely to take matters into their own hands, abandoning one party en masse rather than face the prospect of yet another Conservative election victory. Unless Justin Trudeau turns out to be an inspired leader, his party is likely to be the loser in that exodus. Despite the inertia that we believe will keep the parties apart, at least for now, some senior figures in both camps are talking about a merger of progressive forces. As the Ipsos data show, New Democrats and Liberals seem to think alike. In a twenty-first-century political landscape, their policy disputes may be distinctions without a difference. What matters—or what should matter—is that Canadians be able to vote for a progressive party without that vote being nullified through interparty competition.

Strategists for both parties could also play a crucial role. Losing is boring. At some point, a new generation of political leaders and operatives may conclude that defeating the Conservatives should be the first priority, even if that means accommodation with and even sacrifice to the other party. Either way, one party is likely to become so small and weak that it will be forced to negotiate some kind of merger, or at least co-operative arrangement, with the dominant party. We can't tell you when it will happen. It took Labour from 1979 till 1997 to recover from its funk over Margaret Thatcher, steal her best ideas, woo at least some disaffected Labourites back into the fold, find a young, charismatic leader in Tony Blair, and win an election. We don't think either the NDP or the Liberals will achieve all of that any time soon. But the two parties will eventually merge. Either that or one of them will be relegated to permanent, marginal, distant third-party status, its final expiration simply a question of time. Again, we think the Liberals are at the greatest risk of suffering such a fate.

Whatever the permutations, Canada appears to be moving toward a political system clearly marked by ideological fault lines. As long as the Conservatives remain united, they will hold a powerful advantage going into any election. Unless and until they get their affairs in order, the most that the opposition can hope for is that scandal, poor leadership, or simple voter impatience with the status quo will bring another party to power from time to time, though its tenure is bound to be precarious and its lifespan brief. Progressive Conservatives with long memories can tell them what that's like. It's miserable.

8

Not So Fragile

THE CANADA YOUR MOTHER NEVER KNEW

At the opening of the 2010 Winter Olympics in Vancouver, Canada's official languages commissioner, Graham Fraser, objected to the paucity of French during the ceremony. For columnist Frances Russell, the controversy offered further proof of the dangerous divisions that perpetually threaten to tear Canada apart. "The massive power shift from Ottawa to the provinces over the last 40 years means all these regional and provincial cultural and linguistic divides are testing the bonds of Confederation as they have never been tested before," she wrote. The contest for control over resource revenues "could, at any time, plunge Canada into a national unity crisis every bit as deep and threatening as the Quebec secession crises of 1980 and 1995." Unless progressive political forces co-operated to wrest power from the destructive Conservatives, she concluded, "Canada's status as a 'real country' will become ever more fragile."[1]

What rubbish.

If Russell had watched those Olympics with open eyes, she would have seen her thesis manifestly and triumphantly disproven. Not only did Canadian athletes utterly dominate the gold-medal standings, Canadians across the country exulted in the youthful, urban, forward-looking, polyglot land that has become the envy of the world.

It is an obsession of Central Canada's elites to worry over the fragility of the federation. Canada, they warn, is a tenuous nation with no clear sense of its own identity, riven by linguistic and regional divides that threaten, at any moment, to tear the country apart. Only with the most careful and delicate leadership—of the kind that the Laurentian elites have provided for decades—can Canada be preserved. Every day the Tory wrecking crew remains in office weakens the frayed bonds holding the nation together. Unless the crew is soon dispatched, those bonds will surely sever.

The only problem with this hoary argument is that no one outside the Laurentian elites believes it anymore. Canadians, along with the rest of the world, don't think Canada is fragile. They think, as the *Economist* put it in 2003, Canada is cool.

Consider the following numbers from the Ipsos's poll of citizens in 25 countries about their views of Canada. Eighty-eight percent of the people in those countries, embracing populations as diverse as Russia and South Africa, would like to visit Canada. They know us well enough that 86 percent think we're polite (stereotypes travel around the world); 80 percent would welcome a Canadian into their home for a meal; 81 percent think that Canadians are financially well off (because, compared with just about everyone else on the planet, we are); 62 percent describe Canada as a world economic power (let them think it!); 72 percent think we have one of the world's best health care systems (let them think that, too!); the same number believe we are welcoming to immigrants; 79 percent celebrate our tolerance for people from different racial and cultural backgrounds; while 86 percent of the world thinks Canadians are friendly. And 77 percent think we're cool.

By equally large majorities, Canadians are seen as well educated and hard-working. Non-Canadians trust anything with a "Made in Canada" label on it; they would happily entrust their money to a Canadian bank; they believe (despite evidence to the contrary) that we care about the environment, that we have one of the world's most beautiful landscapes, that we enjoy one of the best qualities of life anywhere in the world, and—most important of all—that Canada is a country where rights and freedoms are respected.

Here's what really matters. More than half (53 percent) of the people on this planet, given a choice of living where they are or moving to Canada, would come here. Seventy-seven percent of Mexicans would, 71 percent of Indians, and 64 percent of Turks. Even 30 percent of Americans would rather live north of the forty-ninth parallel.

That's how the rest of the world sees us. But how do we see ourselves? According to the United Nations *World Happiness Report,* Canadians are the fifth happiest people in the world (after the merry Danes, Norwegians, Finns—*Finns?*—and Dutch). Canadians routinely rank themselves 25 to 40 points ahead of the United States and most countries in Western Europe in economic confidence. When asked if we think our country is generally going in the right track or in the wrong direction, about half of Canadians say the right track. If that doesn't seem like a lot, consider that Canada consistently ranks in the top five countries on this measure out of 24 regularly polled countries in a monthly Ipsos poll.

Add it all up, and it turns out that the rest of the world likes us, and we like ourselves. Big deal. Actually, it *is* a big deal. In a hyper-competitive global economy, being seen as a desirable destination is a major advantage. Nearly one in five global employees would think about moving to another country for work, if circumstances required or permitted it. This is a rich vein of skilled workers that could, if tapped into efficiently and deployed effectively, drive any population-challenged country's economy, like ours. After all, estimates are that between now and 2021, a million Canadian jobs could go unfilled.[2]

The competition of tomorrow is the competition for workers. The smarter countries will work hard to enhance their appeal to others. It could prove their economic salvation—blunting the oncoming, relentless, and potentially damaging friction between generations as baby boomers retire over the next two decades, leaving fewer working taxpayers to support them.

That's a huge problem for China, to take one example.

Thanks to its notorious one-child policy, as the *Economist* noted in April 2012, the country's current fertility rate has dropped to 1.56 children per woman. A population that's replenishing itself needs a minimum birth rate of 2.1. China is running about half a baby behind.

China's *under*population problem is so severe that by 2060, the nation is projected to fall below 1 billion people. Combine that with the problems that an aging population presents for health care and pension demands (by 2020, a third of the residents of Shanghai will be over 60), and you have a demographic disaster in the making. "China will have a bulge of pensioners before it has developed the means of looking after them," the *Economist* concluded. "China will grow old before it gets rich."

China is one of Canada's largest sources of immigrants. But it will probably soon become a major and successful competitor for immigrant workers. The question is: Will skilled workers from India, Africa, and elsewhere want to live there? This is why it's so important that Canada is acknowledged both at home and abroad as being both a desirable place to live and a place that welcomes immigrants. This perception gives and will continue to give this country a huge advantage in the competition for these skilled workers.

———

Over the years, immigration has driven our expansion from east to west, and has fuelled the growth of our major cities, especially Toronto and Vancouver. Today, most Canadians (60 percent) believe that immigration is having a positive impact on Canada, especially in terms of our economy. This is in contrast to much of the rest of the world, where nearly half of the planet's population believes that there are too many immigrants in their country, and that immigrants have made it more difficult for their country's people to get jobs, and have placed too much pressure on their country's public services.

The countries with the most negative view of immigrants are Belgium, South Africa, Russia, Great Britain, Turkey, the United States, Italy, and Spain. Consider the annual population growth and fertility rates for these countries:

Annual Population Growth and Fertility Rates in Countries with the Most Negative View of Immigrants

Country	Population growth	Fertility rate
South Africa	1.4%	(2.6)
Turkey	1.3%	2.14
Canada	1.2%	1.53
Belgium	0.9%	1.65
U.S.	0.8%	2.05
Great Britain	0.7%	1.82
Italy	0.5%	1.38
Spain	0.4%	1.41
Russia	0.1%	1.34

As you can see, the anti-immigrant attitude of these countries is a prejudice that most of them, especially Russia and those in Western Europe, simply can't afford.

Thankfully for Canada, the Laurentian Consensus was pro-immigrant, leaving us with not only a multicultural society, but one that most Canadians welcome. The Laurentian elites wanted to see themselves and to be seen by others as tolerant and compassionate. But New Canada, while also pro-immigration, is more likely to see immigrants as an economic resource. They bring their skills to Canada and strengthen the economy, while Canada in return welcomes the new arrivals and promises to accommodate their cultural and religious needs. Immigration today isn't seen as a compassionate or enlightened social policy. It's just good for business.

Although most Canadians have an enlightened view of immigration, high levels still come with a cost. A recent study by the Fraser Institute says that immigrants who arrived between 1987 and 2004 received about $6,000 more in government services per person than they paid in taxes.[3] Patrick Grady and Herbert Grubel, its authors, argue that the immigration selection process needs to be reformed to align immigrant intake with market needs, rather than relying on the current system of using points to select immigrants.

Federal and provincial governments are retooling their immigration policies to attract young, language-skilled, and job-ready immigrants and to encourage employers to pick applicants who fit their needs, even if they aren't at the front of the line. The new and rapidly expanding Canadian Experienced Class category allows students and temporary workers already in Canada to obtain permanent resident status. Meanwhile, quotas for family-class immigrants, who are often older, with fewer skills and little English or French, are being cut back.

It's enough to make the Laurentian elites gag. For them, immigration is about celebrating our tolerance. It is about Canada being open to the poor and huddled masses of the world. Most of all, it is about a post-colonial "multicultural" Canadian identity, which is about the only identity the Laurentianists have been able to come up with.

But the evolution of immigration policy in Ottawa and the provincial capitals resembles something much closer to what Clifford Sifton had in mind. As you'll recall, for Sifton it was all about settling the West. Canada needed farmers to increase the agricultural production of the country, to solve the railway problem, and to help pay the national debt. Sifton also felt strongly that Canada needed the right kind of immigrants: not city dwellers, but pioneers and farmers. The focus was on finding the immigrants Canada needed, not necessarily on the immigrants who needed Canada.

The descendants of these immigrants, of course, are almost entirely urban. Canada is one of the world's most urban countries. And our vibrant, safe, and amazingly diverse cities act as magnets for this latest generation of economic migrants, who further enrich those cities. In its

2012 ranking of the world's greatest cities, the *Economist* rates Toronto eighth, ahead of London (twelfth) and New York (sixteenth). (The winner was Hong Kong.)

The writers at Canada's *MoneySense* magazine disagree. They rank Ottawa-Gatineau number one among Canadian cities, followed by Kingston and Burlington. Calgary scores twenty-seventh, Vancouver twenty-ninth, and Toronto doesn't make it into the top fifty.

While we're doing lists, we should point out that in 2011, *Forbes Magazine* ranked Canada the best place to do business in the world, followed by New Zealand and Hong Kong. The United States was tenth on the list. According to *Forbes*, with "an affluent, high-tech industrial society, in the trillion-dollar class, Canada resembles the U.S., with its market-oriented economic system, pattern of production, and affluent living standards."

All in all, not bad. Not bad at all.

———

So the country is admired globally, its cities are eminently livable, its business climate welcoming, its immigration levels among the highest per capita in the world, and its social cohesion the envy of other nations. These factors have an impact. They lie behind the increasingly robust confidence that Canadians have in their country and its ability to punch above its weight on the international scene. Fully 86 percent of us believe that Canada has a moral obligation to be a global leader. The world agrees. In an Ipsos survey, 18,000 respondents, including 1,000 Canadians, were asked to rank a series of organizations and countries as being either a force for good or evil in the planet. Canada scored at the top of the list, 79 percent, as an "overall force for good in the world." A strong majority (77 percent) of Canadians also felt the same way about Canada's potential. At the very bottom of the list were the two major Cold War protagonists, the U.S. (54 percent), and Russia (52 percent).

The Great Recession had a lot to do with Canada's strong position. The crisis was a huge boost to Brand Canada. Yes, this country felt the same shudder that shook the global economic system after the Lehman Brothers bankruptcy in September 2008. But we recovered quickly. And as the sovereign debt crisis was passed around the world's financial system like a scorching-hot potato, it seemed to miss Canada. Within a couple of months after the great global disruption, economic confidence in Canada had bounced back—maybe not to the heights seen previously, but enough for confidence in Canada to rival confidence in the world's strongest developing markets.

Canada's financial resilience had much to do with conservative banking regulations—regulations, by the way, that the Canadian Alliance had opposed—put in place by Liberal governments and defended in the face of criticism that the country was turning into a backwater in the world of global finance. In this sense, the Tories just got lucky. It helped that emerging markets, less affected by a slowdown rooted in the developed world, sustained Canadian resource exports. And the Harper government could take some credit for constructing an effective stimulus package that fought the downturn without racking up excessive debt. Regardless, by the end of the recession, Canadian banks were the envy of the world, most developed nations would have killed to have the federal government's balance sheet, Bank of Canada Governor Mark Carney was fending off British efforts to get him to take over the Bank of England—though he would later succumb—and Stephen Harper was in a mood to lecture.

The lecture came in a 2012 speech in Davos, Switzerland, when the Canadian PM wagged his finger at Western leaders about getting their fiscal houses in order.

> "As I look around the world, as I look particularly at developed countries, I ask whether the creation of economic growth, and therefore jobs, really is the number-one priority everywhere. Or is it the case that in the developed world too many of us have, in fact, become complacent about our prosperity, taking our wealth as a given, assuming that it is somehow the natural order of things, leaving us instead to focus primarily on our services and entitlements?
>
> "Is it a coincidence that as the veil falls on the financial crisis, it reveals beneath it not just too much bank debt, but too much sovereign debt, and too much general

willingness to have standards and benefits beyond our ability or even willingness to pay for them?"

There was nothing subtle about Harper's message. He wasn't simply describing the situation in Europe. He was describing Canada in the age of Trudeau. And he was inviting Canadians to feel good about themselves and their accomplishments, in comparison with their troubled international peers.

But it's not just our economic success that marks the contrast between the new and old Canada. It's how we present ourselves to the world. Let's go back to the Vancouver Winter Olympics.

A belief had grown widespread in Canada, over the decades, that too keen a dedication to sport was unhealthy in society. After all, look at those Americans with their college teams and oversized stadiums and athletic scholarships. How vulgar. Apart from hockey, which is tied up in the national consciousness in ways no bureaucrat can unravel, amateur sports were underfunded across the nation, and doing your best and having fun mattered more than winning.

Nothing epitomized this attitude more than the video that the CBC ran every night before signing off, in which insomniacs could watch Greg Joy's triumphant clearing of the hurdle at the 1976 Olympics. The thing was, he won silver. Canada is the only country to fail to win a single gold after twice hosting the Olympics: the 1976 summer games in Montreal and the 1988 winter games in Calgary.

This time, things were going to be different. The sports organizations and the federal government were resolved to see Canada take home medals, and they financed that determination through the Own the Podium program of support for Olympic athletes. Though the program had begun in 2004 under the Liberals, Stephen Harper's Conservatives embraced it and increased its funding. This time, Canada was determined not only to host the Olympics, but to dominate them.

At first, things did not go well. There was the tragic death of Georgian luger Nodar Kumaritashvili during a training run on a track that was thought to be too dangerous. When the competition opened in Vancouver in February 2010, the weather was so warm that one British paper congratulated the International Olympic Committee for situating the games in the only location in the northern hemisphere without snow.[4] There was the collective gasp during the opening ceremonies when mechanical problems undermined the lighting of the ceremonial flame. And why weren't more people speaking French?

Worst of all, Canadians came up short on the medal count time after time during the opening week. Journalists quickly turned on the organizers and the athletes. "Can we just admit that our athletes didn't handle performing under the big microscope very well?" asked CanWest columnist Cam Cole. "Can they admit it?"

Actually no, they couldn't. In the back half, the Canadians began firing on all cylinders, and Canadian fans, both in Vancouver and across the country, were so thrilled and became so loud and so enthusiastic that American journalists began writing without irony about the vulgarity of Canadian sports fans. Sidney Crosby's overtime goal, sealing victory in men's hockey and giving Canada the most gold medals of any nation in any Winter Olympics ever, was the biggest and best sporting moment in a generation.

A letter to the editor in the *Globe and Mail* said it perfectly. "Sorry," wrote Richard Bingham, "we didn't mean we wanted to own the whole podium. Just that bit in the middle."

As for the concerns about French, they quickly faded. But perhaps they shouldn't have. Perhaps supporters and critics alike should have dwelled on the larger message. The fact is, those opening ceremonies reflected a new, Pacific Canada thousands of kilometres removed from the attitude of the old centre of the continent. No one in Vancouver dreams of perfect bilingualism from coast to coast. And in the excitement of the games, Eastern conventions, along with Eastern insecurities, were simply forgotten.

A poem associated with the Olympics contrasts perfectly the old Laurentian Canada and the new Pacific one. It was composed by Yellowknife-born poet Shane Koyczan, who recited it at the opening ceremonies. Hearing it, we couldn't help but think of the famous "Joe Canadian" rant from beer maker Molson. While the two pieces share something in common—they point out that it's *zed*, please, not *zee*—they are otherwise completely different. One is forward-looking, confident, Pacific, new.

> . . . *We are an idea in the process of being realized. We are young, we are cultures strung together, then woven into a tapestry. And the design is what makes us more than the sum total of our history.*
>
> *We are an experiment going right for a change . . .*
>
> *We are the colours of Chinatown and the coffee of Little Italy. We dream so big that there are those who would call our ambition an industry . . .*
>
> *. . . We are not the see-through gloss or glamour of those who clamour for the failings of others. We are fathers, brothers, sisters, and mothers, uncles and nephews, aunts and nieces, we are cousins, we are found missing puzzle pieces. We are families with room at the table for newcomers.*
>
> *. . . We are millions upon millions of voices shouting "Keep exploring."*
>
> *We are more.*
>
> *We are the surprise the world has in store for you, it's true. Canada is the "what" in "what's new?"*
>
> *. . . We are the true north strong and free. And what's more is that we didn't just say it. We made it be.**

---

* Reproduced with the permission of Shane Koyczan. Some of his other works include "Stickboy," "Our Deathbeds Will Be Thirsty," and "Visiting Hours."

Suddenly, doesn't the "Joe Canadian" commercial sound old and Eastern, defensive and insecure—in a word, Laurentian?

Hey, I'm not a lumberjack, or a fur trader.
I don't live in an igloo or eat blubber, or own a dogsled.
And I don't know Jimmy, Sally or Suzy from Canada,
 although I'm certain they're really, really nice.

I have a prime minister, not a president.
I speak English and French, not American.
And I pronounce it about, *not* aboot.

I can proudly sew my country's flag on my backpack.
I believe in peacekeeping not policing,
diversity not assimilation,
and that the beaver is a truly proud and noble animal.
A toque is a hat.
A chesterfield is a couch.
And it is pronounced zed *not* zee. Zed!

Canada is the second largest landmass.
The first nation of hockey.
And the best part of North America.[*]

---

[*] Reproduced with the permission of Molson Coors Canada.

Ironically, the actor pontificating as Joe Canadian is Jeff Douglas, who is now the co-host of CBC Radio's *As It Happens*. Essential listening for the Laurentian elites.

———————

Something else has changed: the way Canadians honour, not only their military, but their past. In this sense, it has become cool to be old-fashioned.

Starting in the 1960s, politicians and pedagogues began rewriting Canada's history to make it less uncomfortable for the French. The unpleasant truth is that Quebec exists within Canada because the British defeated the French in the Seven Years' War, and Quebec was one of the prizes. Perhaps in consequence, from the Boer War to the two world wars to the war in Iraq, Quebecers have opposed foreign entanglements. After all, why sacrifice your sons for the imperialist adventures of a federal government that is, itself, the legacy of conquest?

Quebecers also wanted as little to do with the British monarchy as possible. And so, in a series of acts of appeasement, Canadian history, to the extent any of it was taught, emphasized the Canada that created peacekeeping, that fought against apartheid, that campaigned for the land mines treaty, that contributed to the creation of the International Criminal Court. At every opportunity, monarchical vestiges were eliminated or shoved to the margins. Meanwhile, the Laurentian elites sought to craft a set of national myths, built around the Liberal-created Maple Leaf flag, the Liberal-created social safety net, the Liberal-inspired policies of bilingualism and multiculturalism.

When the Conservatives came to power, they set out to create a few myths of their own. Often as not, this involved retrieving a discredited past. They rewrote the citizenship guide for new immigrants, placing greater emphasis on Canada's contribution to the world wars, to the creation of NATO. The guide portrays Canada as a nation proudly promoting peace but willing to defend freedom.

They rebuilt the armed forces. They robustly celebrated the two hundredth anniversary of the War of 1812, when Canadian militia (but mostly British regulars and Indian allies) beat back an American invasion. The iconic sculpture *The Spirit of Haida Gwaii* by Bill Reid, featured on the $20 bill, was replaced on the new polymer bill by the Vimy Memorial, which Harper twice visited during its restoration. Canada's contribution to and heavy losses in the two world wars have once again, under the Conservatives, become pillars of Canadian history.

And each summer, Harper tours the Arctic. There's something about the place that seems to lift him. He is visibly happier, more open, during these visits, once even commandeering an ATV and hot-dogging it along an airport runway in Tuktoyaktuk. (John Ibbitson was there during the Arctic joyride, in August 2010. When he asked whether the prime minister was authorized to take a vehicle onto a restricted runway, Harper grinned and replied: "I think I make the rules.") Harper also attends the annual military display intended to assert Canadian claims over Arctic lands and waters. From sending CF-18s streaking toward the northern border—in pursuit, it must be said, of phantom threats—to completing the Dempster Highway, first envisioned more than half a century ago, the Conservatives are reawakening the national notion of North.

And if the Conservatives could hardly dismantle the Liberal myths of peacekeeping, public health care, multiculturalism, or the Maple Leaf flag itself, they could at least crowd the shelf a little with icons of their own, even if a few of them had to be dusted off, and even if they wounded the tender sensibilities of the more ardent Quebec nationalists.

Under the Harper government, the Queen is once again "in." The Tories ordered that her portrait be hung in embassies and government buildings. They added *Royal* to the air force and navy. William and Kate were nowhere more feted than in Canada during their tour. And there was money for communities that wanted to sponsor their own celebrations of the Diamond Jubilee.

The Conservatives have even revived a forgotten prime minister. John Diefenbaker had been dismissed as a rogue leader—a renegade in power, as Peter C. Newman dubbed him—afflicted with a fierce temper and paralyzing indecision. It didn't help that he was the first prime minister from Western Canada and emphatically outside the comfort zone of the Laurentian Consensus. (Dief was rooted in Saskatchewan, though, like Stephen Harper, he was actually born in Ontario.) He fired the governor of the Bank of Canada, his government became enmeshed in a grade-B sex scandal with a Soviet spy, and by the end his own Cabinet was in revolt against him.

But the Conservatives are rewriting history, celebrating Diefenbaker as the prime minister who first envisioned the possibilities of Canada's North, and who authored the Bill of Rights that preceded the Charter. There's a Diefenbaker Building on Sussex Drive beside the Pearson Building; there's a John Diefenbaker Defender of Human Rights and Freedom Award; one day there will even be a *John G. Diefenbaker* icebreaker plying the Northwest Passage.

As yet, R.B. Bennett remains unrehabilitated.

Many of the new Tory symbols are partisan and will not take root in the national subconscious. Others, especially those that honour the sacrifices of those who built the nation, may endure. Again, while the Conservatives were the first to successfully tap into the New Canadian zeitgeist, other political parties will also embrace the military, the North, and the youthful pride in the becoming Canada. Such values will no longer be partisan; they will be Canadian. What matters most is that the image of Canada as a nation that succeeds almost in spite of itself is finally dissipating. The relentless Laurentian concern over a national identity, or lack of it, the exercises in nation-building that this lack of national sense of self required, the endless accommodations and compromises and glosses that were needed to make the narrative palatable are no more. New Canada is proud of what Canada has achieved—of what it fought for, what it stands for, what it means to itself and to the world.

We are the true north strong and free. And what's more is that we didn't just say it. We made it be.

Exactly.

9

The Big Shift Means Business

IS YOURS READY?

Canadians who were born in this country are getting older. But we are increasingly a society of immigrants, and many of them are younger. Businesses must build trust—with either of these groups, or with both of them. It's as important as the financial data you crunch, or how well you manage your marketing mix. Building trust means mastering the Big Shift.

The most disruptive force in the world today is public opinion. Capitalist democracy is built on opinionated consumers who now rule the roost and call the shots. And just as individuals seek to build trust in their daily relationships with families, friends, and colleagues, companies need to build trust with their consumers. The more a consumer trusts a business, the more likely it is that she will be able to recall its ads and believe its messages. She will be willing to pay a premium for a product or service, and feel good about it, if she trusts the company that sells it. The more a company is trusted, the easier it is for it to make a profit.

So making a profit means building trust. No trust, no sale. Simple, really. But in a country where both the faces and minds of consumers are changing so dramatically and quickly, how is trust built?

This isn't a get-rich-quick book. But we do have a bit of advice for companies seeking to surf that wave of change. Actually, we have five pieces of advice. We'll call them rules, because that makes them sound more impressive. Mastering these rules will help you and your company exploit the potential of the Big Shift.

Rule Number 1:
Pay more attention to demographic market signals

The last time you drew up your business plan, how much time did you spend addressing demographic changes? Statistical data on changing settlement patterns, ethnic origins, and the age of the consumer market are easily available from Statistics Canada and other sources. Do you sell into the Atlantic Canadian market? Did you know that the average age there is several years higher than the national average? Did you know that's also true in Quebec? Have you taken into account the impact of the Ottawa River Curtain on affluence, needs, and tastes in different parts of the country? There is a growing market segment: older women who suddenly find themselves living alone. Do you know about them?

Does your business sell to every part of Canada except Toronto, which you ignore? Of course it doesn't. What company would ignore the largest market in the country? But if you aren't tailoring your products to newly arrived immigrants from third world countries whose first language isn't English or French, that's exactly what you're doing. Let us remind you: at current immigration rates, we are bringing in a new Toronto every 10 years. What market research have you conducted on these new arrivals? What are their income levels? What are their needs? What are their tastes? How do their affluence, needs, and tastes differ from those of the native-born Canadian of European stock? How do their affluence, needs, and tastes differ, depending on their country of origin?

What do you mean, you don't know? You might as well be saying you don't sell into Toronto!

Rule Number 2:
Don't get carried away by Rule Number 1

In 1996, University of Toronto professor David Foot and his journalist collaborator, Daniel Stoffman, released one of the bestselling non-fiction books in Canadian publishing history. *Boom, Bust and Echo: How to Profit from the Coming Demographic Shift* is a terrific and insightful book. It takes one simple demographic trend—that the Canadian population is aging—and turns it into 238 pages of useful advice for businesses, governments, and individual Canadians on how to prepare for our inevitable future. As Foot and Stoffman tell it, "Demographics explain about two-thirds of everything. They tell us a great deal about which products will be in demand in five years, and they actually predict school enrollments many years in advance. They allow us to forecast which drugs will be in fashion 10 years down the road, as well as what sorts of crimes will be on the increase. They help us to know when houses will go up in value, and when they will go down."

But as good and successful a book as *Boom, Bust and Echo* is, Canada hasn't quite turned out as it predicted. That's because the authors placed too much emphasis on a single demographic trend: aging.

Yes, aging is a critical factor in defining our collective future. That's why Canadian demographers have spent so much time on it. But we don't believe the old aphorism that "demography is destiny," especially if it causes us to focus on a single demographic trend. The market—the public, governments, and other actors—can react to a trend and change its trajectory. Newton's First Law of Motion tells us that the velocity of a body remains constant until it is acted upon by an external force. In this case, the external force that is changing the demographic trend of aging in Canadian society is the immigration policy that the Laurentian elites correctly identified as the best response to the challenges of aging. Immigration policy, then, is a market reaction to a demographic trend that has caused immigrants to choose Canada in a disproportionate number—compared with the number who choose other Western countries—as their new home. Because immigrants to Canada, like all Canadians, have the right to live where they choose, they have blunted the impact of aging on communities where large numbers have chosen to settle. Just as their relative absence east of the Ottawa River Curtain has made those provinces older, their abundance west of it, especially in urban centres, has made those regions younger.

Our point is simply that, while demographic changes hugely affect markets, overly simplistic analysis—say, focusing on only one demographic change, or failing to unpack the implications of that change—can lead us astray.

Let's stay with this for just a bit longer. "The aging of the population will accelerate between 2011 and 2031, as baby boomers reach the age of 65," Statistics Canada observed it its analysis of the 2011 census. "In 2026, the first of the baby boomers will reach the age of 80, an age when mortality is high. As a result, the number of deaths will increase significantly." So maybe this would be a good time to invest in retirement homes.

But you have to be careful. You can't assume that the population of retirees will increase along with the population of boomers over 65. Even defining retirement is a challenge. For most Canadians today, it means the year in which they quit their full-time jobs. But they may continue working at those jobs part-time, or they may take up other jobs, or pursuits that almost qualify as jobs—improving their golf swing, for example. Combine better health with a fluctuating stock market that is undermining retirement income, and polling data suggest that most Canadian workers now assume they won't be retiring until around age 67. So companies that manufacture office furniture, for example, need to think about older backs. Delayed retirement also affects corporate health insurance providers and financial service providers who market retirement savings plans. We need to get ready for the older, less predictable Canadian elderly.

Another place in which demography turns out not to be destiny is in the real estate market. Every week some bank, economic think tank, or other group of august experts issues a report warning that Canada's real estate bubble is about to burst. While a lot of this gloom is driven by world market conditions, the fact that Canada is aging also tends to be factored in. Analysts assume that because Canadians are getting older, they will want to downsize their homes. That is, after all, the economically "rational" way for older couples to offload expenses as they prepare for retirement.

But real estate is aspirational, not rational. You can prove this to yourself: How many empty nesters do you know who decided to buy their dream home once they were no longer supporting the kids? Or who purchased an RV or a time-share? Rational? Perhaps not. Satisfying? Deeply.

In other words, while you need to understand demographic trends, you also need to peer inside those trends.

You need to unpack the assumptions and expectations of a changing consumer base. It's true of older Canadians, just as it's true of immigrant Canadians. If you want to win their trust, you have to listen to what they're saying.

Rule Number 3:
The people you need in your business may not live here

Canadian employers face a growing shortage of the skilled workers that they simply must have if they are to grow. The Canadian Chamber of Commerce describes the shortage of skilled labour as one of the top 10 barriers to increasing Canada's international competitiveness. It's not that Canada has an absolute shortage of workers. We just have too many of the wrong kind, and in the wrong places. Along with Canada's anemic national birth rate, the perverse incentives that keep too many workers happily under-employed in some parts of the country are also depriving Canadian businesses of the workers they need in the places where they're needed. And our educational institutions aren't turning out enough of the workers we need. No one, of course, should be forced into training for work they don't want to perform. And an education in the humanities or social sciences can equip a graduate with skills in critical thinking that ultimately have a market value—or so those of us with such degrees tell each other. The hard fact, though, is that a nuanced appreciation of, say, elite accommodation theory won't get you hired as a veterinarian—and Canada needs veterinarians.

But that's all right; we bring in immigrants to make up for the shortfall in skilled native-born workers, right? Actually, no. First of all, the immigration system is inefficient, thanks to decades of governments, Conservative as well as Liberal, that put short-term political interests ahead of long-term economic needs. Federal and provincial governments are starting to fix the problem. But it could take years before Canada starts bringing in the right mix of workers to meet the needs of the economy. Meanwhile, who are you going to hire?

We need to digress very briefly to prove this point, because it's an important one. Though the Laurentian Consensus was inspired in its decision to grow the population and economy through open immigration, it was indifferent in the actual execution of the policy. To illustrate this point, let's take two specific years of immigration and compare them. As it happens, in both years, Conservative governments were in charge. The first year is 1986, when Brian Mulroney was prime minister of a Progressive Conservative government. The second year was 2010, when Stephen Harper and his Conservative Party were in power. Mulroney's PCs were, of course, every bit as Laurentian in their thinking as the Liberals under Jean Chrétien or Pierre Trudeau. In 1986, Canada accepted 99,354 legal immigrants. They were divided into the following categories: Refugees—19,204 (19%); Economic Class—35,840 (36%); Family Class—42,475 (43%);

Others—1,875 (2%). In 2010, Canada welcomed 280,681 legal immigrants: Refugees—24,696 (9%); Economic Class—186,913 (67%); Family Class—60,220 (21%); Others—1,875 (2%).

Despite the caterwauling from some immigration advocates, Canada accepts three times as many immigrants today as it did in the not-so-distant past. And the overall number of immigrants in each category (including Refugees and Family Class) is up. Clearly, it is far easier for all classes of immigrants to get into Canada today than it was a quarter-century ago.

But although more people are arriving in every category, far more Economic Class immigrants are coming today than during the Mulroney years. The percentage in this category has nearly doubled since 1986, at the relative expense of Family Class immigrants and Refugees. The federal government is reinforcing this trend, through recent changes that deter refugee claimants who don't have a strong case, while reducing the wait for Economic Class immigrants who have job skills in high demand. Provincial governments are also placing an increasing emphasis on targeting nominees who have skills that are in short supply. In other words, immigration policy is abandoning the Laurentian emphasis on compassion and focusing instead on economic advantage.

Even so, there is a skew between immigrant intake and market needs. Too many immigrants, even in the Economic Class, arrive lacking either marketable skills or the certification required to practise them. We could go on about the conspiracy among the professions to limit certification of immigrants in order to protect the privileges and incomes of existing members—it's all quite medieval—but what matters for business leaders is that there simply aren't as many people as they need with the skills they need to grow their businesses. Between 2011 and 2020, the federal government estimates that the following occupations will be among those experiencing the most acute labour shortages.

Labour Shortages Expected between 2011 and 2020

Occupation	Number of jobs not filled
Nurse supervisors, registered nurses	30,942
Health, education, social and community supervisors	13,914
Physicians, dentists, and veterinarians	10,097
Mining, oil and gas supervisors	7,414
Logging and forestry supervisors	3,989

The Canadian Chamber of Commerce says the trucking industry, the steel industry, and the hotel and hospitality sector will also be significantly short of skilled workers.

This shortage is not a challenge just for Canada's governments, which are trying to meet it by refocusing intake on high-skilled, in-demand workers. It's an issue for individual businesses as well. Those that are astute enough should be moving heaven and earth to tap into the global market for skilled workers, now that the federal government's shift in immigration policy is making that market easier to access.

The good news is that Canadian businesses are in a solid position to compete for foreign workers. As previously stated, one in five global workers would consider moving to another country to advance his career. And Canada's relative economic success, compared with the ongoing struggles of the United States and Western Europe, makes us a solid choice for those skilled workers looking to relocate. The global perception (an entirely accurate one) that Canada offers both an enviable standard of living and an openness to immigrants not found among many of our economic competitors gives us a formidable competitive advantage over other developed countries. And delivering on this perception presents a solid opportunity to build trust with long coattails. Immigrants who come to Canada and experience success will be the best salespeople for the potential future immigrants that we still need to attract. They will also be our best resource for accessing the immigrant market. They have the experience Canadian business owners may lack in understanding the affluence, needs, and tastes of their communities.

These are all compelling reasons why, if a lack of skilled workers is a barrier to the success of an organization, it should look overseas. But where to look? The logical focus is on those countries that have skilled workers who are most likely to move. Here are the results of an Ipsos survey on global worker mobility. The percentages are the proportion of workers who said that they are "very likely" to consider moving to another country: Mexico—34%; Brazil—32%; Russia—31%; Turkey—34%; India—28%.

Within that list, only India serves as a top-tier source of immigrants to Canada today. This means that there is a lot of untapped potential in countries that are underused as sources of immigrants. In addition, another potential source of new, skilled immigrants could be emerging—or, more accurately, re-emerging: Western Europe. On the Continent, only 10 percent of workers say that they're prepared to move to find work. But that number could soon be escalating by the month. Too many European countries have a deadly combination of labour policies that are unfriendly to youth, coupled with large pools of unassimilated migrant workers from Eastern Europe, who moved to places like Great Britain and France when their countries were given European Union membership. It's only a matter of time before these people start looking for greener pastures. And many of them are not only well educated and highly skilled, but completely fluent in English, or French, or both.

Two generations ago, Canada took in millions of displaced persons and young workers fleeing a continent ravaged by the worst war in history. Those desperate Europeans became the backbone of the Canadian workforce, making Canada more prosperous and successful even as Canada made them prosperous and successful. Europe may be on the brink of another great exodus. If so, we should be ready to throw open our doors once again.

An important strategy for businesses in search of skilled labour, especially those who need a specific category of worker in quantity, is to establish links with technical schools and other sources of trained workers in other countries, directly recruiting their graduates. In addition, attitudes about how to attract new workers need to change. And recruiters need to understand that the dynamic between source countries and intake countries is being transformed. When it comes to hiring skilled workers in foreign countries, workers over·there aren't competing to win a job with us; we're competing for them with other companies and other countries. The competition for talent from the developing world will only intensify as labour shortages grow among developed countries and as developing countries themselves become increasingly developed, able to offer their own citizens good jobs at good wages, with Mom and Dad close by.

Here's what Ipsos's research reveals about the most important incentives for attracting mobile foreign workers. More than anything else, they're looking for:
- Regular round trip tickets to visit their home country
- Paid language training
- A 10 percent pay raise (a surprisingly modest amount to induce someone to commit to such a life-altering move)
- A guaranteed option to return to a previous position after two years of service. (This is a particularly important inducement for employers who want to encourage global

employees who are already part of their organization to come to Canada.)

Canadian recruiters will need to structure attractive incentive packages to entice to Canada those mobile workers who have a lot of choices about where to settle. The days when we were able to pick and choose from among the world's downtrodden and disadvantaged are coming to an end. Increasingly, Canada and Canadian business are competing in a seller's market for skilled workers. Understanding this simple idea is the first step in building trust with your new workforce.

Rule Number 4:
New Canadians are Canadians first

Bringing in 250,000 or more people year after year is profoundly changing the market for consumer goods and services in Canada. Not in all parts of the country, of course. As we've mentioned, in Atlantic Canada and Quebec, the old playbook still applies. Business there will still need to adjust to a pool of consumers that will grow steadily older, with more of them female. But west of the Ottawa River Curtain, the challenge is to sell to the new Toronto that immigration is creating every decade.

Canadian businesses have precious little information about how to market to new Canadians, and their gut instincts about how to do so are generally distorted by the old assumptions: that there is a French Canada, an English

Canada, and an ethnic Canada; that each market should be treated differently; and that the ethnic market should perhaps be avoided, because it's incomprehensible.

That mindset isn't going to work anymore, now that the so-called ethnic market is becoming the dominant market. Does this mean businesses need a different strategy for every Tom, Pao, or Fernando? Actually, no. Multiculturalism today celebrates those things that make Canada unique in the world, while also paying attention to each source culture's own unique "accent," or take, on Canadian identity. It's about selling by celebrating what makes Canada special, with particular attention to details depending on the target audience.

This was recently and powerfully brought home to Darrell Bricker at a parade. Bricker is an honorary colonel of a Canadian Army reserve regiment, which means he fundraises, organizes community events, and attends ceremonial functions. One parade Bricker observed in June 2012 was for the 337 Army Cadet Corps, the oldest and largest of its kind in Toronto. There were about 150 cadets on parade at Varsity Arena, with their proud families and 337 alumni crowding the stands. What a sight it was—the cadets all lined up in their freshly pressed uniforms and mirror-polished boots, senior NCOs with swords drawn, and the Queen's York Rangers Pipes and Drums providing very martial, and very Scottish, accompaniment. All the symbols of old, Protestant, royalist Toronto were there, in full flourish. Except that about 90 percent of the cadets were non-Caucasian. Most were the children of parents from China, India, or Sri Lanka. The group photo taken at the end of the ceremony, minus the Canadian flags, could have been from a parade in Beijing or Mumbai.

Everything had changed—and nothing. These new Canadians were embracing and commemorating an organization that in just a century had completely altered its demographic composition. Every McKee, Rollins, or Corkery had been replaced by a Wong, a Singh, or a Santos. What hadn't changed were the traditions and symbols being honoured. The military, the pipes and drums, the tributes and fealty to Canada's Queen. For Laurentianists, who tried to strip away Canada's British and military traditions to make newcomers feel less alienated, this makes no sense at all. But as it turns out, new Canadians embrace the 337 Army Cadet Corps, bagpipes and all.

What could be a tougher sell to new Canadians than the Army Cadet Corps? This should tell marketers something. Selling into the "ethnic" market doesn't mean going ethnic. Yes, each culture has its own dos and don'ts. But all Canadians, including new Canadians, want to be Canadian first and foremost. (This is obviously less so in Quebec, which has an added degree of subtlety, but fewer immigrants to market to.) Immigrants are looking to embrace what it means to belong to their adopted culture. They want to buy in, and will, provided everyone else also buys in to what makes this country special. Bottom line: the idea of Canada is a strong selling point. If you want to sell to new Canadians, sell the Canadianness of your product.

Here's another way businesses need to rethink the way they sell into the new Canadian market. A recent Ipsos Reid study found that close to 80 percent of Chinese, South Asian, Southeast Asian, and Muslim Canadians planned to be around water during the summertime: a very Canadian approach to combating the heat. But nearly one in five also said that they can't swim. This is what we mean by selling the Canadian idea but paying attention to the local accent. The same could apply to other outdoor or wilderness activities that are quintessentially Canadian, from hiking and camping to canoeing and kayaking. These activities require a certain amount of personal familiarity with skills many immigrants may lack. So what Canadian sporting goods company or non-profit focusing on safety has launched a campaign to teach new Canadians to swim or handle a canoe? Such a campaign could be good for business and save lives.

In a similar vein, the cottage or cabin or camp (the name changes depending on where you live) market needs to retool for new Canadians. Right now, sitting on your dock with a beer remains a very white, old-Canadian pastime. We know whereof we speak: John Ibbitson grew up in Muskoka, the heart of Ontario's cottage country, and Darrell Bricker owned a summer home in the district.

Who owns cottages or cabins these days? In many places, only the truly affluent can afford the cost. Rising real estate prices and capital gains taxes have priced the once lowly lakeside cottage out of reach for much of the middle class. Yet for those who bought into the market decades ago, or who inherited the property, the cottage remains the treasured retreat for ordinary folks who have more generous and structured vacations: public servants, firefighters, police officers, and teachers. Eventually, however, they will want to sell, as they get older and the headaches of deciding how the children will share responsibility for the property become too much. Given that all sellers hope to maximize profit, the people who will buy their cottages—often with the intent of demolishing the existing building and constructing something much grander—will be richer than the sellers and their peers. Today's public servants, teachers, firefighters, and cops often can't afford the types of vacation properties that their predecessors owned. Unless someone can interest affluent new Canadians in the joys of owning a cottage, the cottage market will eventually suffer. This issue is vitally important for lake associations and local chambers of commerce in communities that are reliant on summer residents for their survival. Again, success depends on selling a Canadian concept but adjusting it to reflect a new Canadian accent.

These two examples—there are many more—show the importance to marketers and sellers of reaching out to new Canadians in markets traditionally dominated by Old Canada and winning their trust. There is another aspect to reaching out to immigrants as well. Research shows that new Canadians, especially Sino-Canadians, are more likely to deal with companies and organizations that are involved within their communities. Helping the poor among them, working with new immigrants on settlement issues, donating to the construction of community facilities, and sponsoring local sporting events, such as cricket matches for South Asian Canadians, can win an organization new friends and potential customers. So now your recreation company has another reason to sponsor swimming lessons and kayak handling for immigrants.

Marketing to new Canadians has its challenges. But with an appropriate calibration of Canadian identity to local accents, along with genuine engagement and trust-building within the community, reaching out to the New Canada offers a rich, untapped potential for Canadian businesses.

Rule Number 5:
Learn from politicians

We know: you hate this rule even before we explain it to you. Politicians levy the taxes that drain away your profits. They enmesh you in the red tape of regulation. And as we've just described, their policies are sometimes so perverse that you may have to recruit your next hire from Bangalore or Manila.

But politicians are in the same business you're in, and they probably do a better job of it than you do. They're in the business of selling values. After all, you don't sell chairs; you sell the value of respecting workers' backs. You don't sell lumber; you sell the value of having a dock that the customer builds himself, with a little help, so that his family can more fully enjoy the lake. Politicians sell values, too—conservative or progressive, pro-growth or pro-equity. They sell, depending on their political party or individual candidacy, value sets with differing emphases on freedom, fairness, growth, compassion, independence, community, and so on. Politicians have been marketing themselves and their value sets since the middle of the eighteenth century. They've gotten very, very good at it.

Politicians probably poll more than your company polls. They probably hold more focus groups than you hold. They tailor their messages to particular markets—older voters, college students, recent immigrants, farmers, entrepreneurs, teachers—more successfully than you do. Even the ones who lose elections do this. Governing parties do all of this and more, because they have all the tools of government at their disposal. Even Apple doesn't have the resources of Canada's federal government (for now).

Sometimes politicians do things for reasons that baffle observers, including other politicians and journalists. They commit acts that seem contradictory or self-defeating. Sometimes, that's because they make mistakes, just as businesses do, by misreading market trends. But sometimes it's because they have information that others don't have, and are acting on that information.

Here's one example. The Harper government, it won't surprise you to hear, values the votes of immigrants, especially middle-class immigrants living in the suburbs. There isn't much that matters more to them. And yet the Conservatives pushed through legislation that severely restricts the rights of people claiming refugee status in Canada. Under the new rules, refugees will have their claims assessed more quickly. The immigration minister can decide which countries are "safe," and new arrivals from those countries will find it virtually impossible to make a successful refugee claim. Refugees who arrive en masse, such as the Tamils who came over on the *Ocean Lady* in 2009 and the *Sun Sea* in 2010, are subject to detention and have little chance of seeing their claims accepted. This made no sense to many observers. How could the Conservatives hope to woo immigrant voters by treating refugees so harshly? The answer, in one word, is polls.

First, internal government and party polling showed that legal immigrants are intolerant of illegal immigrants. After all, legal ones filled out the forms and joined the queue. They are the ones least likely to sympathize with those who jump it. Second, polling data showed that overall support for the government's immigration policies dropped sharply with the arrival of the two ships. Canadians are willing to support open immigration only if they see the system as fair and not subject to abuse. Every news story about the refugee claimant who lives in Canada for years, supported by welfare and public health care, only to disappear from sight once the final appeal is exhausted; every criminal who, it turns out, re-enters Canada illegally after being deported; every claimant from the United States or France or some other first-world democracy where clearly there is no danger of being killed or tortured, damages the overall credibility of the system in the eyes of Canadians. Because the Conservatives now live or die based on the support of immigrants and immigration policy, they moved to correct abuses of the refugee system. They knew there were votes, including immigrant votes, in closing the loopholes.

Business people need to watch politicians because politicians understand the marketplace better than they do. Stephen Harper is prime minister because he and his advisors figured out the Big Shift before other parties did and tailored Conservative messaging and policies accordingly. To the extent that opposing political parties have similar platforms, it's because their internal research confirms broad support for those policies. You can figure out what politicians know by listening to what they say, the values they defend. You can figure out what they know about regional and even local markets by watching how they tailor their messages to those markets. Of course, you could always do it yourself. Ipsos Reid would be happy to take your money. But why not piggyback on the market research that elected officials are already conducting? After all, you paid for it with your taxes.

Sum it all up and you have a new rulebook for business success in post-Laurentian Canada. Sales representatives, marketers, analysts, and CEOs who are still steeped in Laurentian assumptions about Canada and who don't internalize what we're talking about here are in trouble. When they think of somebody in a kayak, they probably still think of somebody young and white. They'll be going out of business soon. Will you?

10

The Decline of the Laurentian Media

WHY IT DOESN'T MATTER IF THE
PRESS GALLERY DOESN'T LIKE STEPHEN HARPER

This is a true story: It is election night, May 2, 2011. In the cavernous hall of Calgary's state-of-the-art Telus Convention Centre, hundreds of ecstatic, raucous Tories are in full tribal bloodlust. The only thing missing is war paint. As the giant television screens chronicle the ranks of Liberals going down to defeat, they cheer each toppled incumbent. The NDP surge in Quebec has them howling their derision at the Bloc Québécois. When the networks declare a Conservative majority government, they let out a primal roar. They know they don't just govern in Ottawa now. They own the place.

At the back, in the dark, rows of reporters bend over their laptops, typing furiously. Most have prepared two stories: Tories Held to Minority; Tories Win Majority. The first story is more carefully written because most parliamentary journalists didn't think Harper would win this big.

The polls had the Conservatives on the brink of a majority government but not over that brink; the late surge of the NDP in Quebec had taken everyone by surprise, not least Bloc Québécois Leader Gilles Duceppe. The Liberals had run a smooth, professional campaign in which Michael Ignatieff had conducted innumerable town halls, excoriating the Tories for their contempt of Parliament and their callous disregard for working families. And Stephen Harper's message—that only he could be trusted to protect jobs and growth; that anything less than a majority and the Liberals and the NDP could combine in an unholy alliance—seemed to most reporters simplistic and vulgar. Besides, he wouldn't grant interviews or take their questions.

But the Tories have their majority after all, and as editors yell over the phone about deadlines that have come and gone, the most senior and experienced political journalists in the country hastily update their copy to reflect the new political reality.

In the midst of it all, one reporter turns to another and says quietly: "I think I'm going to be sick."

One reason that many people within the Laurentian elite aren't aware of how utterly they have been eclipsed is that they haven't read much about it in the newspapers. There's a reason for that. Many journalists—at least, among those who ply their craft in Central Canada—are themselves card-carrying members of the Laurentian elites. These Laurentian reporters and editors are unable or unwilling to acknowledge the great shift in political power underway in Canada because that shift, if it is real and permanent, will weaken their own influence. This is one reason why some journalists, including some within the Parliamentary Press Gallery, strongly dislike the Harper government. (John Ibbitson created a minor storm during the election campaign when, writing in *La Presse,* he used the word *detest* to describe the way some members of the gallery felt about the prime minister. So we'll use the word *dislike* instead, though *detest* is probably closer to the truth.) The feeling, it goes without saying, is mutual.

The lamestream media, as Sarah Palin likes to call them, operate as a sort of echo chamber for the Laurentian elites, comforting them in their decline, assuring them that the rumours of their demise are untrue. Of course, as anyone with Internet service knows, the media themselves are in eclipse. For many, their days are literally numbered. But the band plays on as the water laps over the deck. What else is there to do?

―――――

It is a truism among conservative partisans that most political reporters are small-*l* liberals. This isn't true. It would be more accurate to say that most political reporters, especially those who work in the Parliamentary Press Gallery, are Laurentian. On economic policy they incline mildly toward equity over opportunity. On social policy they are unanimously progressive. (If there is a reporter on the Hill outside the *Sun* newspapers who is openly opposed to gay marriage, for example, the authors have yet to meet him or her.) In foreign policy they are for peace, unless the bad guys are really, really bad.

There are many reasons for this Laurentian attitude toward economic, social, and foreign policy. At university, most reporters took degrees in the humanities or social sciences, where Laurentian perspectives prevail. Those who took journalism degrees—Ryerson in Toronto and Carleton in Ottawa offer the two best-known programs— were taught by professors who live among and embrace the values of the downtown elites in both cities.

While not essential to a successful career on the Hill, command of both French and English is a valuable asset, and one most of its reporters possess to at least some degree. (Francophone media are universally bilingual.) As we observed earlier, bilingualism is a characteristic most prevalent in those who grew up near the Ontario/Quebec or the New Brunswick/Quebec border, predisposing the gallery to a Laurentian world view.

The large contingent of Québécois reporters and Ottawa's location on the Ontario/Quebec border also influence the coverage, which skews heavily in favour of Quebec. Even though the province has had virtually no impact on the national political agenda for years, thanks to its resolute determination to vote only for opposition parties, some columnists on the Hill seem able to write about almost nothing else. This is why so many reporters and editors, when conversing among themselves, talk about Ontario, Quebec, and "the regions."

Many parliamentary reporters also buy into the Laurentian notion that the federal government has the right and the obligation to strengthen the union by promoting "national" (read federal) standards and programs. In their eyes, provincial governments are, in every sense of the word, inferior; their concerns parochial and selfish; their bureaucracies second-tier. Ottawa must lead the way, especially in social policy, and if the Constitution insists social policy is the purview of the provinces, then the Constitution must be gotten around. National programs driven by the federal government not only make for a stronger country; in the eyes of Laurentian journalists, they give reporters something to write about other than the latest delay in purchasing new helicopters.

Using the federal spending power to convince or coerce provinces into adopting federal programs is the preferred method for such nation building. It is how public health care was forged, and national standards in delivering welfare. Most politically aware Canadians know that the Chrétien and Martin governments aspired to a national program of daycare delivery. Most Canadians don't know that while the Liberals were in power, the bureaucracy was also quietly working away on a national education curriculum, to be overseen by a new federal minister of education.[1] Pause, for a moment, to imagine the white papers, the First Ministers' conferences, the protests (especially from Quebec) and other forms of federal–provincial wrangling that such a scheme would have entailed. The press gallery would have eaten it up. Sadly for the editorial writers, the scheme died with the arrival of the Conservatives in 2006.

Laurentian attitudes are practically universal within the bureaucracy—those who are responsible for Atlantic Canada and the West are inclined to wear pith helmets to work—as well as within the gallery and among the academics that journalists most commonly cite. Journalists, academics, and public servants all reinforce each other in their shared convictions. Though reporters like to think of themselves as contrarians, they are in reality as reluctant to be seen as strange or different as high schoolers at a dance.

These shared Laurentian assumptions about what is good for society and what is good for the country lead to a certain uniformity of analysis among journalists on the Hill. The *Sun* tabloids are noticeably to the right of the Laurentian mainstream, though many of their reporters trend to the left of their own publications. (The same cannot be said of the columnists.) The *National Post* is equally conservative, though more thoughtfully so. The *Globe and Mail,* though it is the paper most read by Laurentian elites, is also the paper that devotes by far the most resources to covering the West, with a separate B.C. edition and with bureaus in Victoria, Vancouver, Edmonton, Calgary, and Winnipeg. But a Laurentian mindset can be detected in the coverage of both national papers in at least some stories on most days. Power may have moved to the suburbs and to the West, but Laurentian assumptions in the media continue to identify downtown Toronto, Ottawa, and Montreal ("and, you know, Vancouver is also quite lovely") as civilizational centres and everything else as hinterland, some of it quite barbarous.

The Laurentian mindset is most pervasive at the Canadian Broadcasting Corporation. The loathing for the Corp among many conservatives is unfortunate, because the network operates to very high standards. In quality of coverage, CBC News remains the yardstick by which all other broadcast news organizations are measured. But there is justification for conservative anger, because the CBC's Laurentian assumptions are so deeply ingrained that most of its journalists can't even grasp that what they share is simply a perspective, not an immutable reality. For all its claims of balance, the CBC is genetically incapable of expressing any vision of the country other than the Laurentian. When was the last time you watched a CBC news report dominated by criticism of the federal government for overreaching its constitutional mandate and interfering in provincial jurisdictions? Have you ever seen a documentary asking whether all this concern for the environment and global warming might be overblown? What about that investigative report on unemployment insurance and welfare fraud in Canada, or the abuse women suffer at the hands of male-dominated power structures on reserves?

If you're still in doubt, just listen to one week of *The*

Current on Radio One or a few back-to-back episodes of *Power and Politics* on the Corp's cable news channel, or an evening or two of *As It Happens*, or a Saturday or two of *The House*.

In pursuit of balance, the Corp will invite conservative politicians or thinkers onto its programs. What it doesn't accept—what its producers genuinely don't seem to understand—is that these guests are questioned within the context of a set of Laurentian assumptions so universally embraced that any other perspective is treated as exotic.

No wonder Stephen Harper shows so little affection for the CBC. Or CTV or Global. Or the *Globe and Mail* or the *Toronto Star* or the *Ottawa Citizen* or the Montreal *Gazette*. Early in their mandate, the Conservatives decided that the best way to overcome the Laurentian biases within the Parliamentary Press Gallery was simply to ignore the gallery. After three elections and with a majority government now firmly in place, they have been remarkably successful at cauterizing the gallery's influence.

It began with the diktat that the date and time of Cabinet meetings would no longer be published, and ministers would not be available after those meetings for reporters' questions. At a stroke, the decision negated one of the most important venues for reporters seeking to question ministers. The gallery protested. The protests were ignored.

The prime minister's director of communications at the time—Harper goes through them like Murphy Brown went through secretaries—then decided that she would choose who got to ask questions at media availabilities with the prime minister. Absolutely not, the gallery retorted; reporters will decide amongst themselves who asks questions, as they always have. When the Prime Minister's Office refused to back down, most media outlets began boycotting the "avails," as they're called in the trade. As the months passed, however, the boycott weakened and eventually collapsed.

Journalists treasure foreign travel with the PM, partly because it's the closest thing to a vacation many of them get. But there is also news to be had, sometimes from the prime minister himself, when he ambles to the back of the plane to shoot the breeze with the boys and girls of the press. At least, that's the way it used to be. Harper never ambles to the back of the plane. No breeze has ever been shot in his presence. Nor do his senior staff sidle up in hotel bars for an off-the-record talk that could land an astute (and relatively sober) journalist on page one with a scoop. Travelling with Stephen Harper is a very expensive way to send home a quote obtained after three days of waiting for a press conference at which only two questions may be asked, and which reporters in Ottawa see simultaneously because the prime minister's press conferences are so rare they are almost always televised live.

While the networks hang in for the visuals, newspapers have begun abandoning foreign travel with the PM altogether. Lack of access is one reason. The other is that newspapers in Canada are swiftly going broke.

The death of newspapers was first predicted when television arrived. Like all other media, the dead-tree business adapted itself to the new reality, concentrating less on reporting yesterday's news and more on explaining it. Nonetheless, the culture of newspapers is deeply conservative and resistant to change—a legacy, perhaps, of the days when most papers were family owned, and when unions were so powerful that some proprietors were even prohibited from venturing onto the floors of their own printing presses.

Whatever the reasons, newspapers failed to grasp that the Internet, for all its marvels, was a mortal threat to their existence. The first blows came around 2005, when sites like Craigslist, eBay and AutoTrader destroyed the classified advertising side of the business almost literally overnight. The 2009 recession was another shock, as readers and advertisers decided to save money by cancelling their subscriptions and pulling their ads. The third and potentially fatal stroke came in 2011, when national and retail advertisers—banks, car companies, local businesses—began to look elsewhere. Worst of all, online advertising revenue, which news organizations had hoped would ultimately replace disappearing revenue from print ads, began to decline. There are simply too many places on the Net, and too many different venues—including social media and direct contact with customers—for advertisers to be bothered spending the way they used to on old media.

By 2012, American newspapers were operating with half the advertising revenue they had had in 2000. Newspapers started folding entirely or abandoning daily delivery in major cities: San Francisco, Denver, Detroit, New Orleans. The Annenberg School Center for the Digital Future, a respected shop at the University of Southern California, predicted in the summer of 2012 that by 2017 only four daily newspapers would survive in the United States: the *New York Times, USA Today,* the *Wall Street Journal,* and the *Washington Post.* (We're not that sure about the *Post.*)

Advertising revenues in Canadian papers haven't gone into freefall quite as badly as in the United States, but the trend line is depressingly the same. The result has been a wave of layoffs and cutbacks. Most newspapers have closed their foreign bureaus; parliamentary bureaus are being gradually thinned, with reporters ordered to stay at their desks and work the phones rather than venture into the regions for a first-hand look at what voters are thinking and saying.

The result is a pool of reporters even more insulated from the country and its concerns, with analysis based on outdated Laurentian assumptions, even as the reality changes swiftly on the ground.

These false assumptions were never more on display than during the 2011 election campaign. The opposition parties had combined to defeat the Conservative government over the March budget and over its treatment of Parliament. In fact, the Liberals, the NDP, and the Bloc

Québécois actually succeeded in finding the Conservatives in contempt of Parliament for refusing to divulge the full cost of the F-35 fighter program, and for other misdeeds. It was the first time a government had been convicted of contempt—it could happen only, of course, in a minority Parliament—and Opposition Leader Michael Ignatieff was convinced that voters would punish the Conservatives for such undemocratic arrogance.

The press gallery seemed to agree. For the first week of the election campaign, stories on the front pages and on the nightly news obsessed over the Tories' careful scripting of events: their pre-screening of people invited to rallies and Harper's refusal to take more than a handful of questions from reporters. The election appeared to hinge on the indignation of CBC correspondent Terry Milewski at not having carte blanche to berate the Conservative leader at will.

The Conservatives ignored the carping from the media, focusing instead on their message that only they could be trusted to protect the economy. Harper largely bypassed the large media organizations, granting interviews instead to community and ethnic newspapers and talk radio, where he was happy to take as many questions as the grateful interviewer could think to ask. Meanwhile, a press gallery that is obsessed about the influence and importance of Quebec spectacularly misread voter discontent with the Bloc Québécois and the astonishing surge in popularity of *le bon* Jack Layton. Pundits speculated endlessly on whether the Liberals and the NDP would co-operate after the election to unseat the Conservatives and form a coalition government, without considering the possibility that the NDP, not the Liberals, might become the Official Opposition, making any such coalition unthinkable. The question was moot in any case: suburban middle-class voters in Ontario decided not to take any chances; they combined with their Western allies to deliver a majority to the Conservatives.

Some parliamentary correspondents were so chagrined by the election result that they simply refused to accept it. Early in 2012, Postmedia Network reporters Stephen Maher and Glen McGregor uncovered evidence that a rogue campaign official appeared to be behind automated calls to Liberal supporters in the Ontario riding of Guelph, directing voters to non-existent polling stations. Impersonating an Elections Canada official is a serious offence, and the story grew as complaints came in about similar shenanigans from other ridings. Stephen Harper declared unequivocally in the House that whatever had happened, campaign headquarters had neither authorized it nor known about it. But for some journalists, Robogate—as they inevitably dubbed the story—proved that the Conservatives were guilty of a massive conspiracy to obtain their majority government through fraud. These grassy-knoll types were further emboldened when a judge voided the result in Etobicoke Centre on the grounds that votes had been cast there that couldn't be authenticated.

"Just how many other improperly registered votes got into the ballot box that night?" asked Michael Harris, at iPolitics.com. "How did they get there? Robogate has focused on subtraction or voter suppression—votes that never made it to the ballot box. But what if there was voter addition—votes that got there the same way that stuffing gets into a turkey?"

In the end, the Supreme Court upheld the election result. But for Harris, and for some of his colleagues, the allegations of voter fraud confirmed a deep conviction that the Harper government was illegitimate, that it didn't deserve to govern, and that it could not possibly be in power through legitimate means.

This conviction of illegitimacy has long been a feature in the political coverage of conservative governments. "Lyin' Brian" (as Mulroney was not-so-affectionately dubbed by his many critics) was reviled in a way no Liberal prime minister had ever been. Mike Harris's Common Sense Revolution in Ontario was castigated by many of the same reporters and columnists who today loathe the Harper government. In their eyes Liberal governments may make mistakes—generally by not being sufficiently progressive on social policy—and reporters will expose corruption within any party with enthusiasm. But Conservative governments, in the eyes of Laurentian reporters, are different. Genuinely Conservative governments do not belong in Canada. They do not reflect real Canadian values. Real Canadians don't vote Conservative.

Such visceral distaste for the Harper government from some journalists discredits their bylines. For one thing, it insults the intelligence of readers who vote Conservative. For another, it is a gross exaggeration of Tory crimes or misdemeanours. There is no question that the Conservatives play hardball during elections and in between them. More than once, the party has fallen afoul of Elections Canada and been punished for it (although it was the NDP that got slapped the hardest, for accepting hundreds of thousands of dollars from union "sponsors." The Tories have perfected the art of the political attack ad, and practise that art against their foes with particular viciousness.

But it is ludicrous to suggest that they rigged the 2011 election. Polling data were in line with the election result. The riding of Guelph, ground zero for the robocalls affair, was actually won by the Liberals. And though the Conservatives have used their majority to muscle through a legislative agenda with little regard for parliamentary niceties—the omnibus Bill C-38 that enacted a raft of initiatives in one fell swoop was particularly egregious—it is above hyperbole to allege that omnibus bills or prorogations or closed-door committee hearings move Canada beyond the pale of democracy. The Constitution is still there, and so are the courts. The press, what is left of it, remains free, people still have the right to assemble, and the premiers continue to keep a watchful eye on Big Brother in Ottawa. There are too many countries in the world where brave people risk their lives in the fight for democratic freedoms to belittle that struggle by lumping the Harper government in with the many sordid juntas and dictatorships that litter the globe.

The truth is that even if the Conservative tactics were a model of parliamentary decorum—the notion is, we grant you, hard to conceive—these same commentators would be no less enraged. It is the agenda they abhor, not the means of implementing it. Cutting taxes, relaxing environmental controls, leaving social policy to the provinces, backing Israel, pursuing free trade, tightening unemployment benefits, turning back refugees, toughening sentencing: this is what makes them fume. It's so unCanadian, as they see it. Or at least unLaurentian.

And then there is the ineffable. So many in the press gallery detest (there, we said it) the Conservatives because the Conservatives Aren't Like Them. Conservatives cater to a suburban electorate, rather than to the enlightened elites in the downtowns, where most journalists live. They come from the West, an unknown and hostile land for many Laurentian reporters. Conservatives are not sufficiently concerned about Quebec's delicate sensibilities; they are disrupting the compact between have and have-not provinces; they have turned immigrant voters into dupes—or so think many journalists—who vote against their own interests. They are dismantling generations of carefully wrought foreign policy in favour of their own blunderbuss approach. Worst of all, they never return calls.

For these journalists, it's personal, and it always will be.

———

The media preserve and defend democracy by reporting political events, investigating accusations, and offering perspectives. So vital are they that in Australia the government has pondered bringing in a "public interest test" to prevent a possible hostile takeover of one newspaper chain by a mining magnate. In the United States, there are thoughts of converting great newspapers such as the *New York Times* into charities. European governments already subsidize some media and will be under pressure to increase those subsidies. The news is that important. As PBS concluded in a documentary on the future of newspapers: "Without newspapers, what will we know?"

The media are also businesses, and businesses are routinely created and destroyed by new inventions, changing tastes, and other market forces. "Creative destruction," it's called, and the centuries-old news business is in the grip of it. But we need not despair, however much current conditions tempt us. If information is as important as everyone thinks it is—and how could it not be?—then smart people will pay good money for it. There will always be a market for news.

It may be a much more open market than in the past. Journalists are likely to be less protected in sinecures, less sheltered by their proprietor's profits and their union contracts. Each individual reporter or columnist, or whatever they come to be called, may have to sell their product—what they know that others don't, what they're thinking that others haven't thought—in a forum where judgment is instant, rewards are substantial, and punishment is severe. For many, trying to survive in such a journalistic state of nature will be beyond distasteful. (John Ibbitson shudders at the thought of it.) But there may be no other way to sell the news.

That is down the road. But big changes are just around the corner. Some newspapers and magazines are going to go out of business in the next few years. Free-to-air television will also struggle. Newspapers will throw up online pay walls in an effort to replace lost advertising revenue with revenue from readers. As budgets shrink, parliamentary bureaus will grow smaller; some will disappear entirely. Younger readers already obtain their political news from a proliferation of sources, many of which do a better job of catering to prejudices than getting to the bottom of things. Older readers increasingly will join them, as many newspapers get thinner and less interesting, and stories on the evening news get shorter, fluffier, and cheaper to produce. The digital revolution might not improve either the quality of political discourse or the political literacy of voters. But it's happening, and that's all there is to it.

Meanwhile, as the Liberals and the NDP jockey to see who is really Number Two, the Conservatives will continue to dominate the agenda in Ottawa, ignoring or manipulating the gallery at will, while the Laurentian media grind their dentures.

As national politics polarizes between conservatives and progressives, especially on economic issues, political commentary is bound to polarize along with it. To some extent, this is already happening, with the rise of Sun TV and commentators such as Ezra Levant and Brian Lilley ranting from the right, just as Heather Mallick and Lawrence Martin rant from the left.

Some readers will despair that balanced, objective journalism will be sacrificed in this ideological warfare. But we're betting that smart analysis will always have a market. It doesn't take an informed reader long to realize that nobody's opinion is worth anything. It's what you know that counts.

And anyway, what is often considered balanced and objective is simply a Laurentian writer talking to a Laurentian reader. And that's an ideology too.

11

Things Will Change (1)

AT HOME

Someone who was politically aware in 1980 probably accepted these two situations as grimly unchangeable: First, Soviet Russia would never abandon communism or surrender its Eastern European empire. Second, there was no hope for a solution in Northern Ireland.

It took a little more than a decade for the Soviet Union to collapse. Russia continues to struggle with oligarchs, but all of Eastern Europe is free, and much of it is prospering. It took a few years after the fall of communism for Ireland to settle its affairs, but growing prosperity in the republic and weariness over the incessant killings in the north led to the Good Friday Agreement of April 1998, which marked the beginning of the end of the Troubles. Miracles, both of them, to those who were born into the postwar world.

Things change. The assumptions under which one generation of leaders operates gradually disappear without their even noticing. A new generation recognizes the challenge and the potential of that change, seizes it, and almost overnight, in geopolitical terms, the paradigm shifts and a new order emerges.

This is happening in Canada.

Since the Second World War, Canada's political elites have guided the nation based on certain fixed principles: that the union is fragile; that the duty of the federal government is to bind East, Centre, and West together, lest centrifugal forces tear them apart; that everything from culture to agriculture requires protection from the American behemoth to the south; that the greatest challenge facing the federation is keeping Quebec inside it; that the Canadian way is to blend American capitalism with European corporatism to fashion a society superior to both; that Canada should offer itself to the world as a beacon of enlightened accommodation, a searcher after peace through peacekeeping, a helpful fixer whenever the big players mess things up.

None of those assumptions is valid any more. Canada has changed profoundly from the nation that the Laurentian elites continue to hold in their mind. The changes that we have described in this book have transformed the look of crowds on the sidewalk, have determined which people book moving vans and where those vans head, and have challenged the shared assumptions behind our arguments with each other. This great demographic and cultural shift will also change the shared assumptions on which we base the laws and policies that shape our society. As the Laurentian status quo gets swept away, settled notions of how we should govern ourselves get swept away with them: what we owe one another, how we can make Canada a better place. We would exhaust you and, much worse, bore you if we surveyed the entire waterfront. Instead, we'd like to look at a couple of issues about which everyone seems to assume that the status quo will go on forever, and posit a future, based on the Big Shift, where everything changes.

Walls come down. Peace talks break out. And things get both worse and better for Canada's Indians.

A Weakening Voice

Here's something most people accept as grimly unchangeable: the desperate plight of Canada's Aboriginal people will never improve. No one disputes the impact of the European colonizers on the First Nations. The invaders failed to negotiate treaties when they had an obligation to, and abandoned those treaties they did sign. They consigned Canada's Indian population to remote reserves on land nobody else wanted, and then abandoned them. Later generations of occupying leaders, in a mixture of misguided altruism and rank efforts to assimilate native races, imposed one "solution" after another: forcibly moving entire communities; taking children from their parents and barracking them in residential schools, where many were abused; providing First Nations reserves with the bare minimum to support survival, while ignoring the burgeoning plague of domestic violence and substance abuse.

Native leaders fought back, using the courts and the court of public opinion to demand land settlements; partly winning the right to autonomous governments on reserves; claiming an absolute veto on any major development on disputed land. None of this has improved the quality of life on most reserves, where education levels remain abysmally low and lifestyle-induced diseases such as diabetes and fetal alcohol syndrome are appallingly high. A 2012 task force on native education found that less than 40 percent of on-reserve young people graduated from high school. The national average is close to 90 percent. Diabetes rates on reserves are five times the national average, according to Health Canada, which also reports that suicide rates among Inuit are 11 times the national average and among the highest in the world.

Someone who is politically aware in 2013 might conclude that none of this will change, that the land claims process will continue to grind its way through the courts, enriching only lawyers, that inadequate housing and inadequate education will be the lot of those living on reserves forever. If any change is coming, it's for the worse, as high fertility rates swell the ranks of the Aboriginal population, creating even more challenges that neither Aboriginal leaders nor federal or provincial governments are equipped to meet. With every decade, the native presence in Canada will become more dominant and more disruptive, even as conditions on reserves stubbornly fail to improve.

Not a pleasant diagnosis. Except that it is built on false demographic assumptions. The political influence of the Aboriginal community within Canadian society, rather than growing, is actually diminishing. First Nations and other Aboriginal Canadians are in danger of being drowned by a demographic wave.

Because they don't realize how soon they could lose what influence they have, many Aboriginal leaders continue to believe that they can protect their culture by limiting their contact with the larger Canadian society and by pursuing a set of grievances based on land and other entitlements. They are making a terrible mistake.

The best hope for status and non-status Indians, Métis, and Inuit Canadians who want to preserve their lands and rights and culture is not assimilation with the larger society, but living better beside it. A new generation of Aboriginal Canadians is impatiently demanding change, from their own leadership as well as from Ottawa. Many of those leaders are listening. Life is actually improving on many reserves. It could improve even more if that leadership accepts an evolving reality and seizes opportunity, while there is still time.

The First Nations population is growing rapidly, both on-reserve and off-reserve. The Inuit and Métis populations are also on the march. In fact, if you put it all together, the Aboriginal population of this country is expected to double from 1 million to 2 million between 2001 and 2031. That's a huge increase.

We know why this increase will happen. Aboriginal women used to have a lot more children than other Canadians. Note we say *used to* have. For a population to sustain itself, the birth rate must be 2.1 babies per woman. Back in 1970, after the baby boom, the overall birth rate in Canada was closing in on 2.1. But the Aboriginal birth rate was 5.7. That's three times the replacement rate, which means a rapidly growing young population, which is exactly what we're seeing in the Aboriginal community today.

Today, the Canadian fertility rate is 1.5. We aren't having enough babies to sustain our population. The Aboriginal fertility rate is around 2.3. That's 50 percent higher than the general population, but still only a fraction of what it was 40 years ago. What does this mean? It means that once the current generation matures, the Aboriginal population will stabilize. If the Aboriginal fertility rate continues to decline as swiftly as it has over the past 40 years, the Aboriginal population might even start to decline.

This is happening all over the world, and it's mostly a wonderful thing. Fertility rates are already at or below replacement rates in India and China, in Latin America, in Southeast Asia. As women gain more control over their bodies, as they get better educated and obtain more rights, they start having fewer babies. As families move from the countryside to the city, they also start having fewer children (on the farm kids are a labour resource, but in the city they are an economic burden). And for the first time in human history, more people now live in cities than in rural areas. In fact, the only places on earth where fertility rates are above replacement levels are Sub-Saharan Africa and the Islamic Middle East, and even there we are starting to see signs of declining fertility. We talk about overpopulation, but we don't talk enough about *de*population. By 2040, the global population is actually going to start falling.

Lower fertility signals greater equality for women, and a diminishing planetary population will ease the pressure on the environment and the drain on natural resources. But it will challenge the global economy, since fewer people mean fewer consumers and workers—especially workers who can bolster the pension plans for people who no longer work. Population decline partly explains the long, slow economic decline of Japan, whose numbers have been getting smaller since the middle of the last decade. By 2060, Japan will have lost a third of its current people. Populations are also starting to shrink in parts of Europe, which could be contributing to its economic troubles. But the numbers won't go down in Canada, as long as we continue to have the world's most open immigration policy. By 2030, the Canadian population is expected to be still growing, slowly, with that growth due almost entirely to immigration.

So let's put these numbers together. In 2001, the Aboriginal population of Canada was about 3 percent of the Canadian total, according to Statistics Canada. Today it's around 4 percent. By 2031, it will be between 4 and 5 percent. In other words, the Aboriginal population may grow a little bit, as a percentage of the overall population, but not by much. Then it will level off or even start to go down.

But that overall population will be profoundly different. Think about it: the total increase in the Aboriginal population, from 2001 to 2031, will be equal to roughly four years of immigration. The entire Aboriginal population of the country will be no more than about eight years of intake of these immigrants. The entire First Nations population living on reserves, about 370,000 people, is only about 120,000 more than one year's intake of immigrants.

As we've observed, the great majority of new immigrants are from Asia or the Pacific region. Statistics Canada estimates that by 2013, up to 32 percent of the Canadian population will belong to a visible minority—neither European nor Aboriginal in descent. Now think about *that*. About 4 or 5 percent of the population will be Aboriginal. About a third of the population will be Asian or something else that's non-European.

The skew will be even more extreme in the large cities. In Toronto, 63 percent of the population will be foreign born by 2031. The Aboriginal population in Toronto will be 0.5 percent. In Vancouver, the foreign-born population will be 59 percent. The Aboriginal population will be perhaps 3 percent.

Simply put, the demographic influence of Canada's Aboriginal peoples is set to decline, not increase, over time.

And the nature of the non-Aboriginal population will have profoundly changed. The overwhelming majority of immigrant Canadians now come from countries that were once colonies (India, the Philippines, Caribbean nations) or were victims of imperial aggression (China). They bear none of the Europeans' sense of responsibility for their colonial ancestors. The ancestors of today's immigrants played no part in dispossessing the First Nations of their land; their ancestors were themselves dispossessed.

While this may make new Canadians empathetic to the plight of Canada's Aboriginal peoples, it will not make them feel responsible for that plight. Over time, we can expect to see growing impatience from immigrants with the demands and claims of native Canadians. Not only the demographic influence of Canada's Aboriginal population will decline; its influence within the court of public opinion will as well. Already, attitudes are hardening. An Ipsos Reid survey conducted in summer 2012 revealed that 64 percent of Canadians believe governments give too much support to Aboriginal Canadians. That number is bound to rise over time.

Of course, the rights of a community should not be held hostage to the forbearance of the majority. Canada's native people enjoy constitutional protections that the courts will enforce, whatever people may think. But in our experience, if a population is determined to go one way, politicians will ultimately follow. If, over the coming years, empathy for the hardships suffered by Aboriginal Canadians is replaced with my-ancestors-had-nothing-to-do-with-it indifference and impatience, then the capacity of native Canadians to influence the public agenda to their benefit will decline. As their voices fade in the public space, militancy may increase, promoting a hostile backlash from the broader population. Things could get ugly.

Confronted with these realities, the native leadership has displayed a delusional reaction. As the chiefs met in July 2012 to choose a new national leader for the Assembly of First Nations, their message to each other was emphatic and unchanging: It doesn't matter if there are 30 million occupiers or 300 million; it doesn't matter whether they come from Europe or Asia or Mars. The lands of Turtle Island were bequeathed to the First Nations by the Creator; their right to those lands is absolute; the occupiers have neither the right nor the permission to occupy those lands without the consent of the native leadership.

They can go on telling each other that for as long as they choose; in reality their rights, such as they are, are sliding out from underneath them, never to be won back.

The best alternative, from every point of view, is to reverse the vicious spiral of Aboriginal poverty and declining influence. Problems are so entrenched and so complex, and the federal government's record of incompetence and indifference so depressing, that it can be difficult to know where to start. But experience suggests that better education is the key to improving every other measure of quality of life. If the situation on many reserves is not better than it was a generation ago, then that's because high school graduation rates on reserve are as bad today as they were a generation ago. The debacle of the residential schools gave way to the alternative of handing responsibility for education on reserves to the reserve leadership. But many reserves are too small, and their leaders too indifferent to the importance of education, for proper schools to be established.

There is a growing consensus within and outside the native leadership that comprehensive native education reform must involve creating regional or provincial native school boards, such as now exist or are being established in Nova Scotia and British Columbia. These boards would be responsible for pooling funding, setting capital budgets, hiring teachers and principals, and overseeing a curriculum that protects native culture and language while meeting provincial standards. Provincial governments, which are responsible for educating everyone other than on-reserve Indians, would also become more involved. The Harper government is promising that a new *First Nations Education Act* will be in place by 2014. Some chiefs declared themselves against the act even before it was introduced, and they made a strong case: top-down education reform from Ottawa has never worked and has often been a disaster. But the need for reform is urgent. The large cohort of young Aboriginal Canadians is a potentially valuable resource in an era of growing labour shortages. The timing could not be better for a national push to improve education for Aboriginal Canadians on and off reserve.

The Conservatives have made changes that will ensure the *Canadian Human Rights Act* applies to reserves, and have brought forward legislation to protect the rights of native women, who too often lose out when, for example, a marriage ends and the band council favours the claims of the husband. The Conservatives are requiring band councils to publish their salaries and benefits on the Internet for all to see. Most important, they have declared their intention to allow reserves to convert land to private property if the band population and leadership want to go that route. Native leaders claim that private property violates traditions of communal ownership. In reality, the chiefs are worried about on-reserve land being acquired by outsiders (just as they are worried about losing control of on-reserve education). Regardless, only with property rights can natives develop equity and can on-reserve businesses thrive. Private ownership will also allow native government to impose property taxes.

Many reserves in the southern parts of Canada, especially those close to cities, do relatively well. And a new generation of native leaders is increasingly impatient with their elders' litany of grievances, preferring instead to concentrate on improving conditions on reserves.

But Canada's Aboriginal leaders must be aware that their ability to influence the national agenda in their favour will only ebb with time. The Big Shift is shifting them, too. If they're not aware of this, someone should tell them.

"Common Public Culture?" Say What?

The same Ipsos Reid study that showed a majority of Canadians think government is too generous to natives also found that 72 percent believe that Canada should not let in any more immigrants than the 250,000 or so who currently arrive each year. That's an alarm bell. If Canadian attitudes toward immigration begin to harden, the great social experiment that produced the Big Shift will be imperilled. There are three potential flashpoints related to immigration: jobs, crime, and culture. If the great Canadian post-national experiment is to succeed, the approach of government to all three will have to change.

As we've already mentioned, data reveal that recent immigrants aren't integrating as well into the Canadian economy as previous waves were able to. They are part of the Big Shift, but the shift isn't working for them. There are several reasons for this. The semi-skilled work available to previous immigrants has disappeared. How many thousands of Italians fleeing their ravaged postwar homeland landed in Canada with the proverbial five dollars in their pocket, instantly found a job building the Toronto or Montreal subways or the St. Lawrence Seaway, or at GM or Chrysler or Ford, and began to make lives for themselves? Those kinds of jobs are disappearing from the Canadian economy, which is polarizing between software programmers and cashiers. Too often, the new Canadian ends up behind the cash register, regardless of her qualifications in the home country.

Governments at all levels and of all political stripes are increasingly pursuing sensible, non-ideological responses to the problem. As we've already mentioned, Family Class immigration is declining, relative to skilled immigrants, and those immigrants with the language and job skills most in demand are being moved to the front of the line. Federal and provincial governments are working co-operatively (for the most part) to make it easier for foreign students to stay in Canada, to convert temporary foreign workers into permanent residents, and to move the most promising applicants straight into residency and jobs. Fitting immigrants to the job market should be a simple matter of further fine-tuning the system.

Crime has been steadily decreasing in Canada and the United States since the 1970s for a single reason: fertility rates are declining, which means there are relatively fewer young men than there used to be, and young men are more likely to commit crimes than women or older men. A 2010 study by the Australian Bureau of Statistics revealed that males between 15 and 19 were more likely to offend than any other group (they are almost three times as likely to offend as women of the same age), and that the risk of offence steadily declined for every age cohort after that.[1] A Correctional Services Canada analysis based on 2001 data showed that 13 percent of Canada's population was made up of visible minorities (neither Caucasian nor Aboriginal) and that they represented about the same percentage of those incarcerated or under community supervision. That's great news: new Canadians are no more likely to end up in jail than the ne'er-do-wells of pioneer stock.

But among visible minorities, there were marked differences within races. Asians made up 8 percent of Canada's population, but accounted for only 2 percent of those incarcerated. Blacks, on the other hand, made up only 2 percent of the population, but accounted for 6 percent of those in jail.[2] And the newspaper headlines scream what the statistics quietly confirm: too many gun-related and gang-related homicides involve young black men—raised without a father, with a mother who couldn't or wouldn't keep them in hand—who then drifted into gang life and gang violence.

One simple, if extreme, solution would be to curtail immigration and refugees from countries in the Caribbean and Africa that are marked by violence, and that import the violence into Canada when their citizens migrate here. That, however, is quite impossible. While any proscription would be nation-based rather than race-based, the inherent racial bias of such a prohibition would lead to an inevitable Charter challenge. But changes to Conservative immigration policies could produce something like the same result. By cutting back on Family Class immigrants and stressing both language and professional qualifications, the new rules are likely to maximize immigration from countries with better education systems, including India and China, and minimize influx from poorer countries.

The challenge of integrating black Canadians into the mainstream is part of a broader debate on immigrant culture that is already underway and that could come to dominate the public agenda in the years ahead. The question is simple: To what extent should broader Canadian society accommodate the religious and cultural demands of religious and cultural minorities?

The answer differs sharply depending on whether you are in French-speaking or English-speaking Canada. In the space of two generations, Quebec has gone from a deeply religious to a deeply secular society. While before 1960, 90 percent of Quebecers went to church—almost every one of them attending mass—a Leger poll showed that by the end of the last decade the number had dwindled to 6 percent.[3] In fact, an absence of religion is part of the intangible quality of Québécois society, a delayed inheritance from the French Revolution. (That inheritance also includes a taste for street protests.) It is within that context that the Charest government justified its decision in 2010 to introduce legislation banning individuals from wearing face coverings when interacting with government. The purpose of Bill 94 was not, of course, simply to help officials identify people for security purposes. It was to pander to the xenophobic prejudices of those who want Quebec society kept pure. The bill languished on the legislative agenda (perhaps out of embarrassment) until it died with the election call. Nonetheless, Louise Beaudoin spoke not only for the Parti Québécois but for many within Quebec society when she declared: "Multiculturalism may be a Canadian value. But it is not a Quebec one."[4] That was in response to the administration of the National Assembly's decision to prohibit Sikhs from wearing their ceremonial daggers when entering the building. But that one-size-fits-all dismissal of an open and tolerant society could have applied to any debate within the province about what it calls reasonable accommodation. During the Quebec election campaign, PQ Leader Pauline Marois announced policies—a separate Quebec citizenship with a French-language requirement for those who hadn't been born in the province; banning the hijab and the skullcap for provincial public sector workers, while permitting the crucifix—that would have led to the swift end of any English-Canadian politician's career, along with a swift trip to a human rights tribunal.

Outside Quebec, things are so very different. With no treasured culture to defend, English Canada is much looser about who should be allowed to do what. Sikh kirpans are welcome in the House of Commons—and a good thing too, since there are Sikh MPs in both government and opposition. And tolerance toward immigrants is mandated by the simple fact that there are so many of them. With practically half the population of Toronto born overseas, no politician is going to get elected by vowing to clamp down on religious practices or demanding that religious and ethnic minorities adhere to some dubious standard of citizenship. John Ibbitson recalls being asked a few years ago by an editor at the *Irish Times* to write an essay for the paper on Canadian multiculturalism. Happy to do so, Ibbitson responded, but why? The editor explained: "We have several political parties here, each of which claims to be more opposed to immigration than the others, while you have several parties, each of which claims to support immigration more than the others. We want to know how that can be."

It can be, of course, because Canada is a society of settlers, because English Canada failed to establish itself as a nation, and because the experience of millions of Canadians of different backgrounds living together in the big cities turns out to be not just tolerable, but enjoyable. If nothing else, the food is amazing. And it doesn't hurt that, in the biggest cities, immigrants decide who gets elected.

This doesn't mean that anything goes. As the revised citizenship guide introduced by the Tories points out, newcomers to Canada are expected to fully grasp and embrace Canadian laws and values and norms. But those values and norms are largely Western, rather than specifically Canadian. The most Canadian value, if we could ever make such a claim, is tolerance for others in our shared community.

Still, there are voices of opposition beyond the dark allies that can be found on the Web. One of the most influential is the Centre for Immigration Policy Reform. This is no collection of racists and rednecks—its advisory board boasts such distinguished names as Derek Burney, former chief of staff to Brian Mulroney and Canadian ambassador to the United States; Gordon Gibson, once the leader of the

British Columbia Liberal Party, who headed a task force on electoral reform; and Gilles Paquet, the distinguished University of Ottawa political scientist emeritus (and former sparring partner of John Ibbitson on TV Ontario). In the centre's many publications, and in public appearances by Martin Collacott, a former Canadian ambassador who is its spokesperson, the friends of the centre make three broad points. (1) Immigration, even at its current high levels, cannot reverse the aging of Canadian society. (2) Immigrants often lack the skills needed to fill job vacancies, draining the system through unemployment insurance and welfare rather than contributing to it. (3) The policy of multiculturalism on which rampant immigration is based is a fraud that "appears to have been perpetrated deliberately and cleverly with a view to *eradicating the notion of a Canadian common public culture*, to dissolving Canada's cultural traits into a vast soup, and to shaping Canadians into shapeless selves," as Paquet put it in one paper that appears on the centre's website. (The italics are Paquet's.) He sees this cultural erosion, foisted on a deluded public by manipulative elites, as "a looming major disaster for Canada: an irreversible loss of control of Canada's destiny."[5]

We reject the first two arguments and abhor the third. Certainly immigration cannot reverse the process of an aging society, but by bringing in hundreds of thousands of new arrivals every year, Canada can mitigate that impact. This is why the Canadian population continues to grow, even as other developed nations stagnate or enter population decline.

If immigrants are not acclimatizing well to the Canadian labour market, the solution is to rejig the entry requirements to ensure those new arrivals have the language and job skills needed, as the federal and provincial governments are doing.

The third argument, that politicians and other elites are subverting the "common public culture," is just plain offensive. First off, it embraces the Marxist notion that the public has been and can be systematically deceived by elites. We have much greater faith in the collective wisdom of the body politic. The Laurentian elites guided the country for so many decades through consensus because they knew the bounds of what the public would tolerate. Besides, we are skeptical of any argument in which one elite accuses another of brainwashing the masses. If it sounds as though we are coming to the defence of the Laurentian crowd, in this case we are. Multiculturalism was and is an inspired approach to fashioning a society based on tolerance and diversity. Canadians have embraced the policy because it works, not because they've been drilled to accept what, given their druthers, they would reject. Paquet should give people some credit for knowing their own minds.

The second reason this argument is offensive is that it assumes the 20 percent of the Canadian population who were born overseas are not part of the "common public culture." But of course they are. Immigrants have shaped and even defined Canadian culture from the days of the first European settlers: the French *habitants,* the American loyalists, the British veterans from the Napoleonic wars, the Irish immigrants fleeing famine, the Germans and Poles and Ukrainians and Jews fleeing poverty and pogroms, the Chinese workers who built a railway across a continent, the refugees escaping a ravaged Europe after the Second World War, the Indians and Filipinos who come today in search of a better life, just as everyone who came before was searching—they *are* Canada. What "common public culture" is Paquet referring to that excludes them? What qualifications must we possess to join this exclusive club? On second thought, never mind: whatever this club is, we'd rather not belong to it.

This is what we find so disturbing about such arguments. They allude to some halcyon ideal that immigration and multiculturalism have corrupted, but shy away from saying what that ideal might be, because we all know that it contains or implies the words *Christian* and *white*.

We do not contend that modern Canada is valueless— far from it. People come here by the hundreds of thousands every year because of Canadian values. They are the values of individual freedom and collective responsibility that define all democracies and that are enumerated in the Charter and the Constitution. The Canadian gloss on these values celebrates diversity, forced on Canada because it was an uncomfortable marriage of English and French populations, then embraced by Canadians as it expanded to include new arrivals from all lands. If anyone at the Centre for Immigration Policy Reform is aware of democratic freedoms or

Canadian values that are being eroded by immigration, then they should point them out. We note that in the one place where a "common public culture" is aggressively defended—Quebec—the government willingly tramples on democratic freedoms, such as the right to walk the streets wearing whatever you damn well please, and undermines Canadian values, such as respecting the personal sovereignty of others, in defence of that culture.

But then, as Paquet himself unhappily notes and as Ibbitson told Irish readers, this debate is already settled, thanks to the Big Shift. Immigrants preserve pro-immigration policies by voting for politicians who support those policies. And there are now so many immigrants that they can swing elections, just as they swung the election of 2011. Obviously, we believe policies of high immigration and multicultural diversity are tremendously good for Canada. But whether for good or for ill, they are entrenched and unstoppable. Unless, of course, supporters of the "common public culture" would also limit the right of immigrants to vote.

A Conservative Revolution; a Progressive Response

There are elements of the Big Shift that are inherently conservative in nature. They will lead to conservative reforms in social policy, such as health care and education. With about 40 percent of the population—many of them Westerners, many of them immigrants—believing that government is more of a problem than a solution, and with this group voting as a block for the Conservative Party, changes are inevitable. Consider, for example, charter schools.

These schools have their operation funding paid for by governments, like any other public school, but they are run by independent, non-profit corporations. John Ibbitson visited one school that has produced astonishing results. At Amistad Academy in New Haven, Connecticut, the students are almost entirely African American and Hispanic. When the academy first opened, most of them were reading several grade levels below where they should have been—students who essentially were lost within the typical American public school system. But by grade 8, these same students were posting among the best test scores in the state.

The secret is structure, and an obsessive attention to the needs of the student. Teachers usually aren't unionized, and are promoted or dismissed based on how well they serve the students. Discipline is strict and uniforms are mandatory, along with summer school, a longer school day, and an endless battery of testing to assess abilities and measure progress. For many students, school becomes a safe, well-ordered alternative to sometimes chaotic home lives—a place where adults devote themselves entirely to their needs, a place where they are promised that everything is possible but expected to work hard to achieve it.

Charter schools usually have to rely on philanthropists for capital funding, and often must make do with fewer dollars per child than equivalent public schools. Some charter schools are badly managed. Teachers' unions are fighting them to the death, and many state governments have blocked or slowed conversions from public to charter schools. Nonetheless, the astonishing success of many charters shines through. In the District of Columbia, which has one of the worst-performing school systems in the United States, more than 40 percent of students are now being educated in charter schools, as parents simply give up on the regular public system. Graduation rates in D.C. charter schools are 24 percent higher than in regular public schools and eight percent higher than the national average.[6] When Hurricane Katrina devastated the New Orleans schools system, which was legendary for its incompetence at educating the city's poor black population, civic officials decided to use the opportunity to innovate. Almost 60 percent of the schools in the Big Easy are now charters, and the results simply cannot be denied: A rigorous assessment of 44 charter schools in New Orleans by Stanford University found that 23 were outperforming their conventional counterparts; another 12 were doing as well. Nine were underperforming; three of these had already handed in their charter.[7] One great advantage of charter schools is that those that fail can be quickly closed or have their management and teachers replaced.

The steady mountain of evidence in favour of charter schools made Barack Obama a convert to their cause, despite his close ties to teachers' unions. From being virtually non-existent in 1999, charters have burgeoned to more than 5,000 schools, educating 5 percent of American students. In the U.K., since David Cameron became Conservative prime minister in 2010, more than 2,000 "academies," as U.K. charter schools are called, have opened. The Liberal Democrats strongly support the new program. The education minister, Michael Gove, imported the idea, not from the United States, but from Sweden, where "free schools," are hugely popular.

The commitment to the charter school movement by liberal governments and political leaders, and their dedicated purpose of improving the quality of education for students from poorer families, should make them a favoured cause of the left. But because they rely heavily on testing, and because they are fiercely opposed by teachers' unions, charters are seen as a conservative education reform in Canada and are banned everywhere but in Alberta, where the few that exist cater to gifted as well as challenged students.

We believe that the proscription on charter schools in Canada could be about to shift. Asian immigrant voters have little time for the union-cosseted approach to teaching. The conservative mindset of Westerners favours strong curriculums and standardized testing over the fuzzy and feel-good nostrums still embraced by much of the Central Canadian education establishment.

The need for charters isn't urgent or widespread in Canada. Because we have avoided developing a racially defined underclass outside the Aboriginal experience, we don't have extensive ghettos and underperforming schools. Overall, the public education system serves middle-class Canadians pretty well. But Aboriginal Canadians on and off reserve are not being served. Inuit graduation rates are an appalling 25 percent.

In our large cities, housing projects and high-rise suburban mini-ghettos feed the gangs that generate so much gun violence. Charter schools aren't always the best solution. But a strong, emphatic, and state-directed approach to fighting gang violence among black youth is the goal, well-funded and closely supervised charter schools could be a large step in that direction. The notion that the welfare of anyone—teacher, parent, politician—other than the student should matter in education is immoral. We expect to see the pressure for charter alternatives increase as impatient voters demand solutions to the challenges of those Aboriginal, immigrant, and visible-minority children who aren't getting the education they deserve and desperately need.

We expect to see pressures for other internal changes thanks to the Big Shift. We expect to see demands for private-sector alternatives in health care, as an aging and immigrant population tires of the queues. We expect to see increased pressure from the West and Ontario to limit equalization components in federal transfers, and increasing pressure to rethink the equalization program itself. The equalization formula comes up for renewal in 2014. With

Ontario a "have-not" province, there will be great pressure to rejig the formula so that once again only provinces east of the Ottawa River Curtain benefit from it (and Manitoba—a bit). But the Harper government will stay loyal to its elected base, capping funding increases so that taxpayers in "have" provinces aren't dinged any more than they are now to support those in the "have-nots." This will only further increase pressure on those east of the curtain to reform their sclerotic economies, unless they want to watch ever-more of their taxpayers heading down the road.

We expect to see Employment Insurance gradually revert to its original intention of insuring against temporary job loss, rather than as a welfare-in-all-but-name program for economically depressed regions. We also anticipate demands for fewer regulations, with market principles trumping social concerns. The Big Shift in power to the West and to suburban immigrants will make Canada inexorably a more conservative place.

But the right won't have things entirely its own way. The more Canada tilts in that direction on social policy, the greater the pressure will be for the left to unite in reaction. We see evidence of that shift in one area already: Stephen Harper has made environmental issues sexy again.

The science of global warming is beyond the scope of this book, though we accept the overwhelming body of evidence in favour of a manmade contribution to rising temperatures. But regardless of the science, global warming as an issue of concern to voters is dead in the water.

Environmentalists lost the fight to convince Canadians that they should sacrifice to save the planet not long after Al Gore picked up his Nobel Prize in 2007. Ipsos polling at that time had 27 percent of Canadians naming the environment as their number one concern, second only to health care. The economy tied with education for third, chosen by 13 percent. By January 2012, the two main issues had changed: the economy was the number-one issue and the environment had dropped to number four.

Issues of Top Concern to Canadians

Issue	Oct. 2007	Jan. 2012
Economy (General)	13%	28%
Healthcare / Medicare	29%	26%
Jobs / Unemployment	3%	17%
Environment	27%	16%
Education / Schools	13%	10%

Notwithstanding the fact that they fought and lost the 2008 election on the issue of a carbon tax, the Liberals and their Laurentian allies continue to argue that the Harper government has abandoned its responsibilities to combat climate change. It certainly has, going so far as to formally withdraw from the Kyoto Protocol in 2012. And then the Conservatives went further, streamlining environmental assessments in order to speed approval of natural resource infrastructure projects and attacking environmental groups that opposed the Tory agenda, claiming they were fifth columnists for foreign interests with a "radical agenda." When the environment was at least registering on the public consciousness, the Conservatives made noises about implementing a cap-and-trade system that would limit industrial CO_2 products, with overperforming firms able to sell credits to laggards at the market-clearing price for carbon. But the recession put that scheme on the back burner, and the Tory majority win put it on ice.

After the 2008 election, the Liberals converted to promoting their own cap-and-trade system for reducing CO_2 output by taxing industrial emissions. But the Tories had done a better job of capturing the public mood. Rather than focusing on fighting carbon dioxide, they seized on tangible issues: tackling smog, cleaning up polluted lakes, setting aside new national parkland. Consumers are willing to put up with higher gas prices in exchange for greater fuel efficiency and cleaner air. What they won't pay for, or put their jobs at risk for, is a scheme to lower carbon dioxide emissions to keep the planet from warming up. The more the Laurentian/Liberal/environmental coalition beat the global warming drum, the more ordinary voters turned up the stereo. Which is what makes Thomas Mulcair's Dutch disease argument so devilishly clever.

Mulcair may or may not succeed in yoking industrial workers in Ontario to nationalist, socially progressive voters in Quebec. As we've explained, we think not—at least not right away. But the NDP has at least succeeded in yoking the pipelines to the environment, which could be to Stephen Harper's cost.

More than one prime minister has been brought down by hubris over infrastructure. With John A. Macdonald, it was money to stave off his political opponents so that his precious national railway would go forward. C.D. Howe's determination to build the TransCanada Pipeline by invoking closure on the legislation needed to approve it did in the St. Laurent government. Now Stephen Harper is determined to cement Canada's future as an energy superpower by selling oil sands bitumen to the world. But that's easier said than done. The Obama administration's decision not to approve the Keystone XL pipeline, at least temporarily, frustrated plans to increase sales into the U.S. market. As an alternative, the Harper government aggressively pursued the Northern Gateway pipeline, which would send oil to Asian markets via an Alberta-to-the-Pacific line. The regulatory hurdles were steep, so the Conservatives dismantled many of them. Environmental groups vowed war, so the Conservatives demonized the environmental groups. First Nations groups are powerfully opposed: the Conservatives are building a case that they consulted as best they could, which they hope will clear the bar when the bid to block the pipeline inevitably reaches the Supreme Court. Thomas Mulcair didn't have to demonize Harper as a reckless exploiter of natural resources, willing to sacrifice jobs and the environment to placate his business buddies. The prime minister made the case all by himself.

The sorts of citizens who might have voted Conservative in the past but who aren't married to the party began to wonder whether Stephen Harper was going too far in his relentless drive for pipelines. Suddenly, the NDP was competitive in the polls with the Conservatives. Suddenly, the first glimmer of a strategy that could bring the government down appeared on the distant horizon. By and large, the Big Shift is good for conservative causes. But not all causes, and not all the time.

Our only point is this: The Big Shift is real and permanent. The coalition of suburban middle-class voters in Ontario and voters in the West is powerful. If the Conservatives are to be defeated, progressives must take the Big Shift into account. They must take the changing attitudes of immigrants into account. They must take the West into account. If the Conservatives are to be defeated, they must be defeated *on their own turf*. Rallying the votes of students and faculty at the University of Toronto, bringing Montreal's student protestors onside, recruiting labour leaders (without actually recruiting factory workers), and co-opting the Occupy movement will not elect a government. By talking to one another about one another and then convincing one another that they are the majority, downtown progressives delude themselves. Get into the suburbs. Go west. Win your arguments there. And then you'll be in government again.

12

Things Will Change (2)
ABROAD

It's called a grip-and-grin. Two politicians meet, shake hands, smile at the cameras, exchange a few pleasant words of greeting. In this instance, Canadian Prime Minister Stephen Harper and Chinese Premier Wen Jiabao stood in the Great Hall of the People as a marching band and an honour guard strutted their stuff. Then the leaders repaired to a side room, where Wen offered what was supposed to be the standard welcome-to-my-country boilerplate.

"This is your first visit to China, and this is the first meeting between the Chinese premier and a Canadian prime minister in almost five years," Wen told Harper through an interpreter. "Five years is too long a time for China–Canada relations, and that's why there are comments in the media that your visit is one that should have taken place earlier."

Jaws dropped. It was unheard of for a Canadian prime minister to be so firmly rebuked by another foreign leader.

(Old hands will remember Lyndon Johnson raging against Lester Pearson for criticizing the U.S. bombing campaign in Vietnam. Johnson grabbed Pearson by the lapels and yelled: "You pissed on my rug!"—but at least that was in private.) Criticism of Harper and his insufficiently respectful attitude toward the Middle Kingdom duly appeared in newspapers and on television the next day—clearly part of a Chinese strategy intended to humiliate Canada's prime minister.

There was more to come throughout the trip: greetings at airports by minor instead of major officials; dinners where Harper was placed beside the wife of some second-tier politician, just to show how little he mattered.

Harper bore it stoically. He knew he was being punished, and he knew he had to accept the punishment if he was to repair the damage he had inflicted through his disastrous China policy.

The Conservative prime minister had failed to learn his own lesson. Harper and his advisors were the first to grasp that shifts in wealth, population, and ethnic makeup were transforming Canada, and that a new conservative coalition was theirs for the crafting. But Harper was, in every sense of the word, a domestic politician. He had rarely been outside the country and, apart from a passionate commitment to Israel that he embraced in his teens, had given little thought to foreign affairs. Moreover, he was beholden to the strongly conservative base that had taken the leadership of the Canadian Alliance away from Stockwell Day and given it to him. He had asked for patience from those core supporters as he negotiated the union with the Progressive Conservatives and fought to unseat the Liberals. Harper had reined in the Reformers' bent for social conservatism in order to appeal to the largest possible electorate. On foreign policy, at least, he could throw them some of the red meat they craved and deserved. Besides, he had similar appetites himself.

When he took office, Harper was determined that Canada would distance itself from the godless communist regime in Beijing—going so far as to personally boycott the Beijing Olympics—and would support brave little Taiwan and the courageous struggle of the Dalai Lama for Tibetan freedom. His government would come down four-square on the side of defending Israel, right or wrong, cultivate ties with Latin America to counter the Liberal dalliances with unsavoury Asian regimes, ignore the corrupt and ineffectual United Nations, and place its faith in closer ties to the United States—the only ally in the world any good conservative should really want to have. The striped-pants set at foreign affairs, Harper resolved, would be put in its place. Canada would have a principled and proudly conservative foreign policy.

It was all horribly wrong. Worse, it was stupid.

Harper's strategy completely underestimated the rising economic and geopolitical power of China. It ignored the rising power of the other Asian giant, India. It grossly overestimated the willingness of Latin American countries to develop closer ties with Canada. It misread the labyrinthine lines of power in Washington, where a senator from an affected state can have far more power over an issue—softwood lumber, anyone?—than a president.

Worst of all, from a Conservative perspective, it was bad domestic politics. It insulted Chinese and Indian immigrants, the very voters Harper was counting on to grow and sustain his conservative coalition. And as the business community heatedly reminded him, it was bad for business, especially Western-based resource businesses looking to open new markets in Asia.

The education of Stephen Harper on foreign policy has meant, at times, a complete reversal of his earlier priorities. It has meant getting smarter in linking relations with countries overseas to domestic considerations. It has meant putting up with insults from his Chinese hosts. It has meant mastering the Big Shift all over again.

It has not, however, meant a reversion to Liberal and Laurentian foreign policy principles. Over the years, Harper has mastered the art of tailoring a new image of Canada in the world, which the world couldn't care less about but which plays increasingly well at home. He has married the emerging nationalism of the New Canada to his own partisan ambitions. He has even, along the way, learned to be a statesman now and then.

Probably in no other field of endeavour have Conservative policies left the Laurentianists in greater anger or in greater despair. But once again, if they are to unseat the prime minister, they are going to have to internalize the same lessons Stephen Harper has learned and turn those lessons to their own ends.

Canadian foreign policy will one day not be so conservative. But it will never again be Laurentian.

A Stronger True North

A kid with long hair and a backpack with a small Canadian flag makes a call on a cell phone. An old man answers.

"Hello, Grandpa."

"Mark!" The old man beams. "What a nice surprise."

The kid tells his grandpa he's in France.

"*Aaah*, Paris." The grandfather smiles. "Are the girls still as lovely as I remember them?"

But his grandson isn't in Paris. He's in Dieppe. "I guess . . . I guess I'm calling to say thanks, Grandpa."

The old man weeps. So do we.

This is a television ad, an old one for Bell cellular service. Since it first aired in the 1990s, it has reminded us that Canada has a history far different from and richer than the politically correct one of the more recent past. And Canadians, even younger ones, are grasping to reconnect with that history. This the Harper government is helping them to do with a vengeance, as it redefines the Canadian past and the Canadian myths through, of all things, the country's military.

Anyone who watched the long and lamentable decline

of the Canadian Forces from the 1960s through the 1990s should be astonished by this. For years, for decades, militarism was passé in Canada, and the military a source of mild, and at times acute, embarrassment.

The Laurentian Consensus view of the military was shaped by the 1956 Suez Crisis, an abortive attempt by France and Britain to seize control of the Suez Canal from the upstart leader Gamal Abdel Nasser. The operation failed thanks to the incompetence of its planners and the outrage of the United States, which had not been consulted and which reserved the right to replace unfriendly dictators with people more pliant, if circumstances required.

Canada's external affairs minister of the day, Lester Pearson, earned the Nobel Prize for his efforts to broker a ceasefire through the use of United Nations peacekeepers, as they came to be called. And that's what Canada became—a post-colonial good guy, with no imperial or territorial ambitions, friendly with the great powers but sympathetic toward the little fellas of the developing world, always willing to lend a peacekeeping hand.

But not much of a hand. After the Second World War, becoming a soldier was not something the son of a Laurentian elite was expected to aspire to. Money was needed for the ambitious suite of social programs that were the much preferred mission of Liberal governments. Quebec had always been suspicious of overseas military adventures, and Pierre Trudeau and Jean Chrétien seemed wary of, even hostile to, the military and its demands. Equipment was allowed to become antique and force levels to diminish, so that funds could be diverted to health care and other programs. British Prime Minister Edward Heath fumed that Canada in NATO was willing to give "all aid short of help." Later, the Forces paid the price for eliminating the deficit through even tougher budget cuts. Under Chrétien, defence spending in Canada fell to 1 percent of GDP, seventeenth in the NATO alliance, just ahead of mighty Luxembourg.[1] Canada's soldiers became (poorly) armed aid workers, symbols of our moral superiority and ineffectual commitment to peace and security. Despite the fact that Canada was a middle power in name more than reality, governments maintained just enough military strength to keep us in NATO and earn an occasional seat at the table when the world's players sat down to talk.

The situation left John Manley, who was foreign affairs minister in the Chrétien government, lamenting: "You can't just sit at the G8 table and then, when the bill comes, go to the washroom." Manley made those remarks shortly after the attacks of September 11, 2001. And though the Laurentian elites did everything within their power to ignore, or at least mitigate, the consequences of that terrible day, the truth is that Canadian foreign and defence policy divides neatly into the Laurentian policies that preceded it and the post-Laurentian world that Canada is part of today.

Peacekeeping, in principle and in practice, was a failure. Most of the 30 missions achieved little, endangering the lives of our soldiers while failing to prevent the violence they were supposed to contain, but allowing Canadians to feel good about themselves while conveniently earning Canada chits at the talk shops of the foreign policy community. Some missions were chronic (think Cyprus, which lasted 29 years), some catastrophic (think the horrors of the Balkans), and some misguided attempts at humanitarianism that blew up in our faces (think Somalia).

And then there was the nightmare of Rwanda, the ultimate genocidal failure of under-equipped United Nations peacekeeping troops, lacking either mandate or support, who were forced to watch as Hutu militia slaughtered between 800,000 and 1.1 million Tutsis, Hutu moderates, and Twa Rwandans over 100 days. No wonder the mission commander, Canadian Lieutenant General Roméo Dallaire, suffered a collapse and tried to take his own life six years after the end of his mission in Rwanda. His warnings and his recovery—he now sits in the Senate—offered an object lesson to all Canadians on the terrible decline of the peacekeeping mandate and the complicity in slaughter into which Canadian troops were being forced.

There were accomplishments. Canada was a major force behind the Ottawa Treaty to ban landmines and the creation of the International Criminal Court. And following the Rwandan genocide, the United Nations adopted the doctrine of Responsibility to Protect (R2P), which gave other nations the right to intervene if a state was unable or unwilling to protect the lives of its own citizens. That doctrine was a Canadian initiative, co-authored by one

Michael Ignatieff. Lloyd Axworthy, another of the Chrétien government's foreign ministers, proudly referred to the Canadian approach as "soft power." But American officials quietly scoffed at Canadian pretensions. Joseph Nye, an American scholar and advisor in the Clinton years, had coined the term. But soft power—the ability of a country to influence other nations through its moral and cultural example—has meaning only if there is adequate hard power in reserve. Otherwise, soft power is simply pointless moralizing.

However badly equipped the missions were, however lacking in equipment and mandate, however disastrous the outcome, Canadian public opinion was largely with the Laurentianists on peacekeeping. It was how we saw ourselves in the world. We were the good guys. Unlike the Americans, we were there to help. This was especially the case during and after the Vietnam War. We were striped shirts and whistles, not players in the game.

All of that changed after 9/11. An enraged America demanded real help from its allies. Canada, suddenly aware of its own vulnerabilities, began to rearm. The quasi-pacifist Chrétien government that had offered only token support in Afghanistan and had refused to join in the quagmire of Iraq was replaced with the more militant government of Paul Martin. But when Martin found himself in mortal political peril, he reflexively reverted to the Laurentian mantra of anti-Americanism. Martin reversed his support for the Bush administration's ballistic missile defence program, and abandoned his initial boosterish approach to national defence. Instead, the Liberals pivoted, or perhaps just returned to form, warning that the Conservatives would squander money on guns, when the real need was for butter, in the form of a national child care program.

It all climaxed in a 2006 campaign ad (which made it to air but did reach the inboxes of journalists) that contained this remarkable narrative:

Stephen Harper actually announced he wants to increase military presence in our cities.

Canadian cities.

Soldiers with guns.

In our cities.

In Canada.

We did not make this up.

Choose your Canada.

Actually, they did make it up—Harper never proposed any such thing. And it missed a larger point. Canadians had a new respect for their military, for the sacrifices they were making in Afghanistan, for their new mandate to make the peace, and not just keep it. The ad represented an absolute disconnect between the values of New Canada and Old Canada. Over the last decade, the only major profession in Canada that has experienced a significant increase in public trust has been soldiering. It's up 17 points from the mid-seventies, according to Ipsos Reid tracking surveys. The military are now up at the top of the list, with first responders. In contrast, national politicians have continued their search for the bottom and are now in single digits in terms of trust, rivalling car salespeople. Those politicians, however, have been responsible for rearming the military, especially the army, which shouldered the burden in Afghanistan. By 2012, spending on the Canadian Forces had reached 1.4 percent of GDP, still well behind Great Britain (2.6 percent) and France (2.3 percent), not to mention the United States (4.7 percent),[2] but enough to create what one general, speaking off the record, described as a "splendid little army."

The personification of this newfound respect for Canada's military, at least in English Canada, is the 172-kilometre Highway of Heroes. The route runs from CFB Trenton to the Centre of Forensic Sciences in downtown Toronto. During the Afghanistan campaign, Canadians lining overpasses along the Highway, sometimes in the most unspeakable weather, to pay tribute to fallen soldiers returning to Canada were a frequent sight.

Initially, the federal government and the military wanted to keep the return of the dead from public view, fearing it would inflame antiwar sentiment. But people got word anyway and came to the Highway of Heroes to pay their respects. As one former general told the authors, "That was when we realized that the Canadian public had taken ownership of their military."

Walk into any coffee shop or restaurant or rest stop on a major Canadian highway with a Canadian soldier in uniform—especially in a town where there isn't a strong military presence. See how long it takes for someone to thank the soldier for his service, or to offer to buy her a coffee or a meal. While our soldiers appreciate the recognition (and the coffee), they still can't quite believe it. Too many remember that it wasn't long ago when they were told not to wear their uniforms off the base or on public transit lest they be met with public hostility and harassment. But things have changed.

The Education of Stephen Harper

Increasing funding for the military, and standing four-square behind it, aligned Stephen Harper's government with the public will. It was one thing he got right from the start. But he got other things terribly wrong, especially in the all-important matter of trade. It took three wasted years and a complete U-turn before the Conservatives managed to get this country's trade policy on track. In essence, Harper finally learned and applied the lessons of the Big Shift to foreign and trade policy, just as he already had on domestic issues such as crime and taxes.

Harper's first priority was to thaw the serious chill that had set in on Canada–U.S. relations. There was a host of irritants, and not just over Canada's refusal even to offer moral support for the conflict in Iraq or its reversal of support for missile defence. The Americans had erected a plethora of non-tariff barriers at the border, slowing the flow of goods and people across the border. Local protectionist concerns were part of the issue, but the real problem was the threat of terrorism. The administration of George W. Bush was powerfully suspicious of the hundreds of thousands of people from third world countries who settled in Canada every year. As one rather drunken Homeland Security official explained to John Ibbitson at a Washington social function in 2008: "You guys let in a whole lot of people, and you don't know who they are." There was also the problem of softwood lumber. The Americans had slapped tariffs on Canadian imports, claiming timber licences on crown land were subsidized. The Canadian side won in the courts, but the courts have little power over a senator determined to protect local interests from Canadian competition. The Bush White House kept promising remedies but, as many Canadian prime ministers have learned to their sorrow, Congress has easily as much power as the administration within the American system, and convincing Congress was a much tougher deal than convincing an American president before or after the smiling photo op.

The Harper government was able to reach a deal on softwood largely through the efforts of David Emerson. Emerson had made a career of switching: from the senior ranks of the British Columbia public service to the banking industry, back into the public service, back to the private sector, this time in forestry.

He switched again to run federally for Paul Martin's Liberals in 2004, ending up as industry minister, and was re-elected as a Liberal in the 2006 election. He then shocked the nation by switching to the new minority Conservative government before Harper was sworn in and becoming minister of international trade. Emerson didn't care who his boss was; he just wanted to get things done. The first thing he wanted to get done was an agreement on softwood. The final terms were very much to the Americans' advantage—Harper was just starting to learn how hard the Americans play ball—but it was the best Canada could get, given political realities south of the border. After that, Canada–U.S. relations went on hold as this country joined the rest of the world and most Americans in waiting for George W. Bush—whose irresponsible tax cuts, deficits, and calamitous handling of the war in Iraq had made him one of the most toxic presidents in history—to finally leave.

Meanwhile, Harper and Emerson had other priorities. Though there was much the new prime minister needed to learn, he was right in intuitively grasping that the time had come for the Canadian government to jettison its Laurentian tradition in foreign policy.

Since the Second World War, Canada had been a good and faithful ally of anything multilateral. We were present at the creation of both NATO and the UN, and while Canada's contribution to the military alliance became more of an embarrassment with each cut to the armed forces, the country was always available for at least token peacekeeping duties when the UN asked for help.

In trade policy, the wonks at Fort Pearson emphasized

a firm attachment to multilateral institutions. Trade was, in fact, as much about foreign affairs as it was about jobs for Canadians. Canada supported trade liberalization through the General Agreement on Tariffs and Trade (GATT) and its successor, the World Trade Organization, and buttressed that support by generally avoiding bilateral deals. The one initiative that split the Laurentian Consensus wide open was Brian Mulroney's decision to pursue free trade with the Americans. Many within the Consensus saw no alternative to a rising wave of protectionism within the United States. Others believed it would mark the beginning of the end of Canadian sovereignty. The Liberal Party under John Turner fiercely opposed the agreement, leading to the watershed election in 1988.

While the Chrétien government reluctantly reversed itself and endorsed the 1993 NAFTA accord that brought Mexico into the tent, the Liberals continued to favour multilateral over bilateral agreements. The problem was that the Doha Round of global trade talks bogged down over the question of agricultural subsidies. With no new bilateral agreements to speak of, and with the WTO unable to bridge national divides, Canadian trade policy stagnated.

Emerson was determined not to wait for Doha to sort itself out. He launched an ambitious set of trade talks with non-EU European nations and with several Latin American countries. Then he moved to negotiate an agreement with the European Union itself. Staff at International Trade began to complain about being worked to death.

Meanwhile, the folly of the Harper government's China policy was becoming clearer by the day. In 1997, 1.4 percent of everything imported into China came from Canada. That number steadily declined, bottoming out at 0.97 percent in 2006 before modest growth resumed. The economic crisis of 2008–09 and its aftermath reinforced the error of Harper's ways. Between 2007 and 2011, the Canadian economy grew by an average of 2.5 percent annually. The United States economy, which was savaged by bank failures and falling real estate prices, managed only 1.7 percent growth. Great Britain did even worse: 0.7 percent. By contrast, during the same period, Chinese annual growth averaged 9.1 percent. And it wasn't just China. India's GDP rose by 6.9 percent, while Brazil posted a respectable 2.7 percent.[3]

Stephen Harper was getting educated. The United States, while it would remain the world's most powerful economy for years to come, was grappling with crippling deficits and political gridlock the likes of which hadn't been seen since the Civil War. Canadian trade with the U.S. had already fallen from a high of 84 percent of Canada's total exports in 2002 to 72 percent in 2011, according to Statistics Canada. Europe's high taxes and anti-business bias were coming home to roost. An emerging block of powerful no-longer third world nations would set the economic agenda in the decade ahead. And Canada wasn't on its radar.

Even more important, from the Conservatives' perspective, Harper's foreign policy was angering the very voters he needed most to grow his base and possibly form a majority government. Immigrant Canadians had already started to drift away from the Liberals; as we saw, by 2008, new Canadians were almost as likely to vote Conservative as Liberal, the first sign of the shocking shift. But Harper's contemptuous attitude toward these voters' home countries wasn't helping his cause. The nature of Chinese immigration had changed. In 1980, 56 percent of Chinese immigration to Canada came from Hong Kong, mostly affluent émigrés worried about what would happen to their money after the former British colony reunited with China. But by 2010, 97 percent of immigrants came from the mainland. While they might not have had any great love for the government in Beijing, they lacked the Hong Kongers' antipathy toward it. Harper's criticism of China, and his refusal to show up at the Olympics, disrespected the Chinese immigrants' mother country and their people. Indo-Canadians were no less miffed at the indifference, even outright neglect, of Ottawa's approach to India.

So the Harper government's foreign policy was skewed in favour of declining powers, it antagonized rising giants, and it angered key domestic constituencies. What was good about this? Nothing, the prime minister realized, and he began to shift. Cabinet ministers were dispatched to China; new consulates were opened there and in India. And in autumn 2009, Harper went on his first grand Asian tour. He endured the snubs in Beijing, got manhandled by Sikh security at the temple at Amritsar, gawked at the fabulous wealth of Shanghai and Hong Kong, gazed pensively across the demilitarized zone at North Korea, and set in motion what would turn into a plethora of trade negotiations: with India, with China, with Thailand, with Japan.

"I think we have every reason to believe that the markets in the United States and in Europe that have been our more traditional market will probably experience slower growth for some time to come," Harper told reporters in Seoul in 2009 at the end of his Asian excursion. "So the greater opportunity is obviously in the Asia-Pacific region."

He added that Canada was uniquely positioned to profit from the rising tigers, because of its natural resources and because of the millions who had come to Canada from these very countries in recent years. He might have added that he was uniquely positioned to profit from this about-face by reaping Asian-Canadian votes.

Back on this continent, the arrival of Barack Obama in the White House—he was more beloved by Canadians than by his fellow Americans—opened up new opportunities. The two governments agreed to integrate border security and customs clearance procedures to thwart terrorism and improve trade. A decade ago, a continental security perimeter would have produced howls of outrage over lost sovereignty. But the Beyond the Border agreement prompted barely a murmur. New Canada realized that a nation's sovereignty resides elsewhere—in its sense of itself, in its presence before the world.

But truth be told, BtB, as it was called by wonks, was a bright light in what was increasingly a darkening landscape along the forty-ninth parallel. Faced with powerful labour and environmental interests within the Democratic Party and an implacably hostile Republican Congress, Barack Obama found the Canada–U.S. relationship an easy lamb to sacrifice. The sacrifice started small, with Buy American provisions that froze Canadian companies out of bidding for contracts under the recession-fighting stimulus program. It got much, much, much bigger when the administration caved to pressure from environmentalists and failed to approve the Keystone XL pipeline, designed to carry oil from the Alberta oil sands to American refineries. Approval, Harper insisted, should have been a "no brainer."

And then chagrin turned to genuine anger on the Canadian side as the Americans demanded severe concessions from Canada before allowing it to join the Trans-Pacific Partnership talks. The TPP itself was another part of Stephen Harper's education and a powerful demonstration of the Big Shift in action. A small free trade agreement among a few Pacific nations began to expand as other countries expressed an interest in joining. Then the United States signed on—in hopes of increasing exports and, some alleged, to contain Chinese influence in the region—and suddenly the TPP talks were heading toward creating the world's largest free trading zone.

And Canada wasn't a part of it. When first approached, back in 2006, the Harper government was indifferent, unwilling to join unless the other TPP partners agreed in advance that supply management was off the table. This was the decades-old system that protected the Canadian dairy and poultry industries from foreign competition through a system of quotas and tariffs. Though dairy and poultry were hardly key strategic industries, dairy farmers, especially, were a vocal and powerful lobby, especially in Quebec and Eastern Ontario. Laurentian governments, both Liberal and Conservative, had agreed that dairy cows were sacred cows. The Harper government was equally willing to sacrifice trading interests for domestic votes. It was extortion, pure and simple, but it worked.

But the recession and the rethink on Asia and the Pacific also caused a rethink on the TPP, especially after the United States joined the talks. Here was potentially the biggest trade deal on the planet about to be signed, a vast trading zone stretching from Australia to the U.S. to Vietnam, and Canada was on the outside. And so Stephen Harper, now fully educated, once again reversed himself and began to press other governments to let Canada into the TPP talks.

The key was getting the Americans onside. The prime minister and his advisors were confident that the goodwill created through the Beyond the Border agreement and the personal chemistry between the president and the prime minister would ease Canada's accession to the talks. But the Americans turned out to be the hardest sell of all. Though Canada was finally offered its seat in June 2012, the negotiations were so bruising, and the final terms so humiliating—Canada was, in essence, allowed to join only as a second-tier member— that the Harper government was left grinding its teeth. Derek

Burney, a former Canadian ambassador to Washington, and Fen Hampson, a respected scholar on Canadian foreign policy, were not speaking only for themselves when they wrote in *Foreign Affairs*, the bible of the American foreign policy establishment, that the Obama administration's actions had "brought U.S.–Canadian relations to their lowest point in decades. . . . If the pattern of neglect continues, Ottawa will get less interested in cooperating with Washington. Already, Canada has reacted by turning elsewhere—namely, toward Asia—for more reliable economic partners."[4] The Americans knew that that this was Ottawa talking.

Nonetheless, by the end of 2012, the sea change in the Harper government's foreign policy was fully in place. The Latin American initiative fizzled. Canada could not get into Mercosur, the Latin American free-trading zone, without the support of Argentina, whose wacky government (the governance of this country, which a century ago was as prosperous as Canada, has been a sad mixture of the tragic and the farcical for many decades) was determined to keep foreigners out rather than let them in. Although Brazil was clearly a rising power, hopes for a Latin American economic miracle had proved premature. Besides, there weren't that many Latino voters in Canada. They preferred the United States, which was warmer and where their extended families could often be found.

Instead, Canada was firmly launched on a new trading relationship with the EU—though its value was questionable, since the continent was more of a source of economic crisis than of economic opportunity—and on multiple initiatives with Asian and Pacific nations. Senior Conservatives quietly acknowledged that they considered success on the trade front as the yardstick by which they would measure themselves. If Stephen Harper was to have a legacy, other than slaying the Liberal Party, trade would be it.

In a way, it's actually all very Laurentian. For decades, old-school nationalists have argued for a separate Canadian destiny beyond its umbilical attachment to the United States. Trudeau's Third Option sought to broaden and deepen trade links with Europe and Asia exactly as the Harper government is doing. One difference is that Trudeau wanted to wean Canada from an excessive dependence on the United States, a country he simply didn't like very much, especially when Republicans were in charge. Harper instead is forced to diversify trade because of a weakening United States. Another difference is that Trudeau's Third Option was intended to appeal to Laurentian anti-American nationalists. Stephen Harper's trade agenda, at least so far as domestic politics is concerned, appeals to Asian immigrant voters. A third difference is that the imperatives of globalization have compelled this federal government to at least consider dismantling trade barriers that were as much about political parochialism as about economic interest.

Regardless of circumstance and motivation, it will be a supreme irony if Harper, the Yankophile, succeeds where Yankophobic Laurentianists failed in weaning Canada from trade dependence on the United States.

Trade diversification, however much the Laurentianists themselves wished for it, is going to be a serious shock. The hypocrisy of the Laurentian approach to trade was rooted in its dependence on American forbearance. As Canadian trade diversifies, Canadians will discover that other markets are not nearly so forbearing.

The Americans were willing to look the other way at the tariff walls around poultry and dairy. They grumbled, but accepted prohibitions on foreign ownership of financial services and cultural industries. Old-school Canadian nationalism denounced the swaggering imperial power to the south, while counting on its military to protect Canadian interests, its capital to finance Canadian investments, and its politicians to look the other way as federal governments cossetted industries that economic nationalists insisted had to be protected for the sake of national identity.

But how are these protections to be sold to the Chinese and the Indians and the Australians and the Vietnamese? The argument is hard enough to make convincingly at home. Apologists for supply management maintain that quotas ensure a safe, reliable supply of dairy and poultry products while protecting family farms without government subsidies. That's perfectly true. It's the consumer who subsidizes the industry, through higher grocery bills. Why family farms are to be preferred to larger corporate farms is a question of romance and nostalgia rather than reason. As for the contention that, without supports of some kind, Canada could become reliant on foreign exports, putting our national food security at risk—what the heck is food security? Are these subsidy apologists predicting some kind of apocalypse that will leave the people starving unless dairy farms are close at hand?

Canada's new trading partners will be indifferent to these arguments, whatever their merits. Twenty-first-century globalization is uninterested in local arguments for local protection. The Trans-Pacific Partnership talks are showing us that. Expanding into Pacific markets will mean abandoning quotas and caps. The Americans may have done Canada a service by forcing such tough conditions on the Harper government before allowing it into the TPP talks. They served notice to vested interests that the next chapter in Canada's trading relationship with the world will involve dismantling remaining tariffs. It won't happen overnight. Farmers will need compensation and that compensation won't be cheap. Foreign ownership restrictions on banks and telecoms will need to be lifted gradually. As Canada reorients from the Atlantic to the Pacific, from North America to Asia, there will be disruption and destruction—most of it creative; some of it unavoidably destructive.

The Laurentian elites can be counted on to fight for their sacred cows. What's a point or two of GDP growth here or there when the soul of the nation is at stake? Except it was never about the soul of the nation. It was about protecting votes in rural ridings. It was about keeping mercantilist Quebec happy. It was about preserving a certain sense of Canadian culture that disappeared round about the time that the most popular Canadian authors began signing six-figure advances, Canadian painters dominated Australian art exhibits, and Canadian singers started headlining in Las Vegas.

Resolutely Principled, When Convenient

Stephen Harper was appalled. He was in Cartagena, Colombia, at the Summit of the Americas, where Latin American leaders were pushing for a resolution supporting Argentina's claims to the Falkland Islands, which that country had invaded and been expelled from by British forces 30 years before. There was nothing new in Latin American solidarity on the question of the Malvinas, as Argentina calls the islands. Except that Barack Obama was calling them the Malvinas, too, and was signalling support for the resolution. The Americans had always been officially neutral on the question of who owned the islands, and the American president wanted to co-operate with his southern neighbours if he could.

We absolutely must not support the resolution, Harper urged the American president at the conference. It was for the islanders to determine their fate, he reminded Obama, and they were determined to remain British. This was a matter of deep principle for Canada, Harper maintained. Obama came around and backed Canada in opposing the resolution.[5] The resolution failed.

Cristina Fernandez was livid. "This is pointless. Why

did I even come here?" the Argentinean president was over-heard protesting as she left the conference.

So it's not that the Conservative foreign policy has become entirely subordinate to economic concerns. (Though it might not have been entirely coincidental that Argentina had frustrated Canadian ambitions on the Latin American trade front.) If trading relations are not at stake and there is no domestic constituency involved, the Harper foreign policy can be deeply principled. But that principle is almost invariably at the service of domestic political needs.

What that principle isn't is nuanced. What it isn't is multilateral. What it isn't is soft. What it isn't is Laurentian.

For those elites, Canada has lost the subtlety, sophistication, and bona fides in foreign affairs that helped us blend in so well among the world's smarter salons, righteous NGOs, and esteemed faculty clubs. To the Laurentian Consensus, moral certainty in a complicated world is the act of a simpleton or an ideologue. To them, the New Canada, especially Stephen Harper and the Tories, qualify as both.

The Canadian foreign policy elite was born out of Canada's evolution from dominion to nation. A fraternity of brilliant and erudite men—Lester Pearson, Hume Wrong, Norman Robertson (the three are buried beside one another in a Wakefield, Quebec, cemetery), and their colleagues and successors were present at the creation of the United Nations and NATO, active in negotiating ceasefires in the Middle East, at the forefront of Canada's recognition of China (well ahead of the U.S.), working quietly behind the scenes to help soften the collapse of the Soviet empire and the reunification of Germany, involved in Balkan and African diplomacy, essential to getting a landmines treaty, and much else beside.

The diplomats at foreign affairs were, and are, an elite brigade, quietly certain they understand the nuances of geopolitics better than their political masters, not so quietly dismissive of anyone who thinks otherwise.

Except they are Atlanticists, and the nation is reorienting itself toward the Pacific, along with the government of the day. The diplomats are more concerned with geopolitics than trade; they are committed multilateralists, where the Tories are more focused on the key alliances of the anglosphere. And they are dismissive of domestic political considerations, while the Conservatives obsess over them. The two just don't get along.

This was never more poignantly brought home than on the memorable day in March 2010 when Robert Fowler gave his speech. The former Canadian diplomat has had a 38-year career in the federal public service. In that time, he was a foreign policy advisor to prime ministers Trudeau, Turner, and Mulroney. He was also Canada's longest-serving ambassador to the UN and represented Canada on the Security Council. He is perhaps best known for having been kidnapped and held by al-Qaeda in the Sahara when he was serving as a special envoy for the UN secretary general.

Fowler re-emerged on the public stage because of his temper tantrum at the "big ideas" conference Michael Ignatieff and the Liberals held in Montreal in March 2010. At the conference, Ignatieff and his fellow Liberals were treated to a tongue-lashing by Fowler, who intended his criticisms as much for the governing Conservatives as for the Official Opposition. (The Conservatives were wise enough not to give him a platform.)

Fowler focused his vitriol on Canada's recent failure to be elected to a rotating seat on the UN Security Council (the apex of global importance for any self-respecting member of the Laurentian elites). Said Fowler: "We no longer represent the qualities which we Canadians have long insisted candidates for the council should bring to such responsibilities. The world does not need more of the kind of Canada they have been getting."

What got Fowler's dander up? Mostly, it was the Harper government's "endorsement of Israel, right or wrong, [which] has meant selling out our widely admired and long-established reputation for fairness and justice in the most volatile and dangerous region of the world—the Middle East." All in an effort, Fowler said, "to lock up the Jewish vote."

Here was the Laurentian Consensus in full moral outrage. Fairness and justice require complexity, studied ambiguity, and courting of both the Israelis and the Palestinians. That means a heavy reliance on multilateralism and doing nothing without the permission of the Security Council.

It also means, for the Laurentian elites, quietly asserting Canada's moral superiority over the United States; our tradition of peacekeeping over invasion; our embrace of soft power and the UN. Once again, Trudeau is held up as an icon, the exemplar of Canada making its own way in the world outside the American shadow.

Certainly the botched effort for the Security Council seat was a cock-up. Harper at first ordered officials not to push hard for the seat, and certainly not to make any deals. Then, realizing that the UN was, yes, a talking shop, but sometimes a very important one, he ordered a full-court press to earn the votes in the General Assembly needed to win a seat. But Canada started too late, and its full-throated support for Israel in an assembly largely hostile to that country doomed our hopes. We lost the seat to Portugal, though no one back home seemed very upset about it aside from a few downtown neighbourhoods.

The contemporary self-image of Canada, however, at least beyond those neighbourhoods, is considerably less subtle. Certainly the Harper government's strident embrace of Israel speaks to a more black-and-white world view. The same world view was on display when Canada stepped up to help lead the NATO mission that aided the rebels who overthrew Libyan strongman Muammar Gaddafi. A Canadian general led that attack and Canadian CF-18s flew more than their share of sorties.

But in truth, domestic politics is always in play, and Fort Pearson knows it. The Libya mission was popular at home as

Canadians cheered on brave rebels fighting corrupt dictators from Tripoli to Damascus. Harper supports the cause of the Israelis from personal conviction, but that support has also turned several ridings with large Jewish populations away from the Liberals and over to the Conservatives. When it was Canada's turn to chair the G8 and the G20, Harper led an initiative that committed billions of global dollars to improve maternal health in the developing world. But not a dollar of Canada's share of that commitment was to be spent on abortion services. During a visit to Ukraine, the prime minister was blunt in warning its government, which is dominated by eastern Ukrainians of Russian background, that the world would not tolerate the creeping repression that threatened to snuff out the emerging democracy. Of course, it didn't hurt that Canada's large Ukrainian population hails mostly from the western and more Europhilic part of Ukraine.

Canada's role in the world is changing. We have new assets to bring to the table of global diplomacy: a Pacific coastline, large Indian and Chinese populations, natural resources, a beefed-up military, and an increasingly coherent and confident sense of self.

Much of this the Laurentian Consensus helped to create; some of it they can even support. But none of it belongs to them anymore. Conservatives and Westerners and Asian immigrants today speak for Canada in the world. Stephen Harper's education is complete. It was about trade, stupid, and votes at home. For Canada abroad, that's really all that matters.

Conclusion

MARGIN OF ERROR

We wrote this book to start a debate. To be clear, we're not objective participants in this debate. We have a point of view informed by public opinion research, census data, and the years we've spent observing Canadian politics. By this point, some readers may agree with all or part of what we've had to say; some may not. That's fine. People of goodwill can disagree on political questions.

We think of this book as a polite provocation. (We are, after all, Canadian.) We want to get the attention of those people who claim to speak for and about contemporary Canada. As you will have gathered by now, one of our goals was to grab the Laurentian elites, as we call them, by their rhetorical lapels. Because they don't get what is happening to Canada, many of them have, in their frustration, adopted a dystopian vision of our society and its future.

We see something very different. We think the Big Shift is transforming Canada before our very eyes into a remarkable, post-national country whose best days lie ahead, and whose wealth and tolerance will make us an example for and the envy of the world.

Yes, the Big Shift is disruptive. Such a confluence of global and domestic trends is bound to shake things up. Canada's economic success and positive global image, its declining birth rate and aging population, the changing levels and sources of immigration, the increase in globalized trade, the ascent of English as the first truly global language, the decline of Quebec and rise of suburban Toronto and the West as power centres, the emergence of new political coalitions, and the issues that are driven by all of these factors—well, it's a lot to take in all at once. No wonder some people are having trouble getting their heads around it.

Even now, long after the event, many fail to appreciate what a watershed the 2011 federal election turned out to be. The Conservatives have for the first time consolidated a new and decisive coalition of taxpayers, while the NDP has taken the lead in putting together a nascent coalition of progressives. Ground zero for this progressive coalition is Quebec, but it has growth potential in most provincial capital cities, university towns, and among those who feel left out of the new taxpayers' agenda championed by the Harper Tories. The progress of Adrian Dix and the provincial NDP in British Columbia deserves to be given particular attention.

The Liberal Party, which remains dominated by the Laurentianists and their ideals, is in peril, regardless of whom they select as their next leader, though at this time it seems that leader is almost certain to be Justin Trudeau. The party may not be doomed to extinction, but any hope for a swift return to its former glory has long since disappeared. Some form of co-operative arrangement between the Liberals and the NDP may eventually be inevitable. There may be no other way for progressives to effectively challenge the Conservatives. It's a simple question of numbers.

The decline of the Liberal Party is, for us, particularly fascinating, not because we wish it ill. As we mentioned at the beginning of this book, if Canada is a wonderful country today—and we obviously think it is—then we have the Laurentian Consensus to thank for it. Many of their decisions were inspired. From the earliest days, they recognized the vital importance of immigration. They crafted a multicultural approach to absorbing those immigrants that has spared Canada the racial traumas so many other nations endure. Their economic policies were, for the most part, sound; their social policies fostered a humane and decent society. No matter where we live or what our political stripe may be, we owe the Laurentian Consensus, and the Liberal Party through which it often spoke, a great deal. They gave us this country.

But the party and the elites who guided Canada simply failed to recognize what was happening to what they had created. In essence, Canada changed but the Liberals didn't. National politics today focuses principally on economic issues, not national unity. It is value driven and not subject to brokerage politics. Everything that the Liberal Party is, Canada isn't anymore.

We understand how confused, disheartened, and angry this leaves those who continue to believe in that Old Canada. For them, a wrecking crew has taken over government and is destroying everything that once made Canada great: its relentless hewing to the middle ground, its moral superiority over the United States, the national standards and programs established by an activist federal government, a devotion to peacekeeping and nuanced morality in global affairs, a hyper-sensitivity to the needs of Quebec, and a proper sense of embarrassment over the institutions of our colonial past. These ideals are not the ideals of the New Canada; often the government of the day pursues the exact opposite. Yet the truth remains that the government is going to where the country is. The Conservatives are not wreckers; they simply reflect the becoming Canada.

Where to from here? The near future will be bumpy. There's much to sort out: myths to be challenged, oxen to be gored, and a new politics to master. Old institutions and assumptions will collapse, and new ones will rise in their place. We can't say what will pass from the scene and what will replace it, but we believe we have provided a broad outline of the Canada to come.

It will be more Asian and less European, more Pacific and less Atlantic. The West will increasingly become the Centre. The failing protections for old industries will be swept away. The great cities will grow in size and power, while the rural and regional will further wane. Political and economic cleavages will be sharper, as those on the ascendant impatiently demand the power and influence that those on the descendant are unwilling to surrender. The food in restaurants will just keep getting better and better.

But only a fool is certain of the future. If Canadian politics over the past decade has shown us anything, it is the folly of extrapolating too far forward from current conditions. If a Canadian had gone to Mars in 2000 and returned today, she would be flummoxed. "What do you mean, Paul Martin isn't prime minister? He should be finishing his second term right about now, unless some challenger is forcing him out of the leadership. *Who* is prime minister? You mean that pasty-faced wonk at the National Citizens Coalition is running the country? With a *majority?* And with the Liberals in *third?*"

Charlton Heston, on the beach, staring at the Statue of Liberty.

As 9/11 reminded us so horribly, unexpected catastrophes can leave every assumption in tatters. Yet we are impressed by how much Canada has *not* been affected by global events. A few weeks after the attacks on the World Trade Center and the Pentagon, Canadians were once again going about their business, even as the United States was embarking on the war on terror. Canadians were as terrified as everyone else by the calamities that rocked the United States and Europe after the collapse of Lehman Brothers. But while much of the developed world continues to struggle to crawl out of the economic morass of the recession that followed, the Canadian economy was back on its feet after a couple of quarters. (Thank you, Laurentian Consensus, for keeping a tight rein on the banks.) Canada appears to be moving very much on its own path these days. And a good thing, too.

There is one shift that could jeopardize everything we have put forward in this book: changing Canada's immigration policy. An Ipsos Reid poll that showed 36 percent of Canadians believe immigration is having a negative impact on the country is a red flag. Fortunately, 41 percent believe the impact is positive. But if public opinion were to shift decisively against the federal government's open-door policy, then everything Canada is becoming would be jeopardized. Remember, as populations age, developed countries will find themselves competing for the most qualified immigrants. Canada has an enormous competitive advantage in that contest; our diversity is our greatest asset in attracting newcomers. A nativist backlash would bring about demographic shifts even as it heightened social tensions. As we've already observed, the good news is that there are now so many immigrants in Canada, and their political weight has become so important, that any political party that advocated curtailing immigration levels would be courting political suicide. Still, on this vital issue, governments must move carefully and watch closely to prevent any rise in intolerance.

Our arguments and projections assume that the Asian dynamos and other powerhouse emerging economies will continue along a path of robust growth. A major downturn, or any revelation that the Chinese economy, in particular, is floating on a bubble would imperil our prediction for growth based on trade diversification. Whatever bumps in the night might occur, we are confident that long-term demand for Canadian resources, including oil, will remain robust. But if we're wrong, several bets in this book would be off.

And then there is the bugbear of Quebec nationalism. While we see economic concerns trumping any sovereigntist impulse among Quebec voters, Canada has a seemingly limitless and tiresome capacity to revive this dormant issue. Whatever challenges Pauline Marois faces—and they are formidable—the fact remains that a sovereigntist government is once more in charge in Quebec. History teaches us that such governments are always troublesome for the rest of the country. But we remain confident that if Quebec restlessness does re-emerge as an issue, it will be a defensive reaction to decline rather than a confident assertion of strength, making it a very different proposition from previous referendum outings.

Caveats aside then, we believe our portrait of the political landscape is an accurate one—plus or minus 3 percent, 19 times out of 20.

Is it a pro-conservative or a pro-progressive portrait? We think it is neither. *The Big Shift* seeks to map Canada's changing political and social terrain. The Conservatives were the first party to recognize the nature of that terrain and exploit it. The people on the progressive side of the dialectic will one day do the same. They will do it by throwing out the old Laurentian maps and making the Big Shift work for them. They will have learned what the Laurentian Consensus seems incapable of learning: that those who wait for the universe to go back to unfolding as it should will wait a very long time.

Acknowledgements

FROM DARRELL BRICKER

My contribution to this book started as a series of speeches on Canada and Canadians that I've been delivering around the country with my sidekick at Ipsos Reid, John Wright. Over the last couple of years, I started noticing that some of the tried and true points that John and I assumed would resonate with our audiences (we'd make the point; they'd knowingly nod in agreement) had stopped working. I didn't know it at the time, but the main argument of this book was starting to take root: the Laurentian Consensus, and all that it represents, no longer has a defining impact on Canadians.

During the 2011 federal election, I realized that the changes I'd been noticing weren't isolated. They were connected, and what they added up to was that Canadians were experiencing a fundamental transition, and our country and its people were never going to be the same. This was something worth writing about. Thankfully, John

Ibbitson (who had independently come to the same conclusion) agreed with me. That's how this book came to be.

I wish I could say that all of our ideas are unique. But many observers had already commented on different aspects of what we talk about here. None of these people, however, have managed to pull these ideas together as a comprehensive, baseline narrative about the New Canada. That's what we set out to do. Some of the observers and researchers that influenced our thinking receive citations in these pages, but many others—journalists, scholars, public servants, political consultants, pundits, business people, and even relatives (Cal and Joseph)—have contributed to this book in ways that they may or may not be aware of. They are too numerous to mention here by name, but I want to sincerely thank them all for their insights.

Also, I want to thank my colleagues at Ipsos Reid for all that they do to chronicle the Canadian experience. They will recognize much of their work here. And in particular, I'd like to acknowledge the invaluable assistance of Keren Gottfried, who provided background research for the book. Keren also co-authored with me the *Policy Options* article on the Ipsos Reid exit poll that we draw from throughout the book.

Acknowledgements

FROM JOHN IBBITSON

The genesis of my contribution to this book came, in part, from a talk that I was invited to deliver in December 2011 entitled "The Collapse of the Laurentian Consensus," as part of the *Big Ideas* series co-sponsored by TV Ontario and the *Literary Review of Canada*. I am very grateful to both organizations for the invitation, which led to consequences I had not expected at the time.

I am also grateful, as always, to my colleagues at the *Globe and Mail* for granting me the gift of the best beat in Canadian journalism and for the many insights I have stolen from them. Some of the ideas and material in this book were drawn from the Laurentian Consensus talk, from articles in the *Globe*, and from other talks and writings.

As always, none of it would be possible, or worth it, without the love and support of my partner, Grant Burke. And I made my deadlines mostly because Huck the dog sat on my feet and wouldn't get off.

We share a joint debt to John Pearce, our agent, who navigated the agreement, and to everyone at HarperCollins Canada. Our special appreciation goes to Jim Gifford, who edited this book and saw what it could be right from the start, even when the co-authors weren't always sure themselves.

Notes

Chapter 1

1. The preceding paragraphs were adapted from "The Collapse of the Laurentian Consensus," a talk delivered by John Ibbitson at the Gardiner Museum, Toronto, December 5, 2011.

2. Deborah Waddell Robertson, "Clifford Sifton and Canada's Immigration Policy," *British Immigrants in Montreal,* http://www .british-immigrants-in-montreal.com/clifford_sifton_policy.html.

3. The information that follows is based on confidential sources.

Chapter 2

1. John Ibbitson, "Harper Unbound," *Globe and Mail,* April 28, 2012.

2. "Canadians Rate Highly Issues Close to Their Day-to-Day Lives," *Institute for Research on Public Policy,* July 2012, http://www.irpp .org/show_study.php?id=402.

3. John Ibbitson, "Canadians Have Little Confidence in Government to Solve Issues That Matter Most," *Globe and Mail,* July 25, 2012.

Chapter 3

1. Margaret Wente, "Michael Ignatieff Was Right about Quebec," *Globe and Mail,* April 26, 2012.

2. O. Coche, F. Vaillancourt, M.-A. Cadieux , and J. L. Ronson, "Official Language Policies of the Canadian Provinces: Costs and Benefits in 2006," *Fraser Institute,* January 16, 2012, http://www .fraserinstitute.org/research-news/display.aspx?id=2147484095.

3. Canadian Press, "Michael Ignatieff Warns Canadian Unity Is at Risk," April 24, 2012. http://www.cbc.ca/news/politics /story/2012/04/23/ignatieff-national-unity.html.

4. Jeffrey Simpson, "Quebec Has Replaced Alberta at the Margins," *Globe and Mail,* April 25, 2012.

5. Chantal Hébert, "This Discontent Could Have Legs," *Toronto Star,* May 17, 2012.

Chapter 4

1. Dean Beeby, "Federal Study Suggests Relocating EI Recipients to Regions with Labour Needs," Canadian Press, May 17, 2012.

2. Allen Rollin, "East Coast Fears EI Change," QMI Agency, June 7, 2012.

3. Based on information at CBC News, cbc.ca/news/interactives/ budgets-provinces/, and Department of Finance Canada, http:// fin.gc.ca/fedprov/mtp-eng.asp .

4. John McCallum, *Unequal Beginnings: Agriculture and Economic Development in Quebec and Ontario until 1870,* Toronto: University of Toronto Press, 1980.

5. David Cameron, "Yours to Rediscover: A Conversation on the Future of Ontario," Mowat Centre, December 15, 2010, http://www.youtube.com/watch?v=r_XbwnMLyPY.

6. Toronto is far more ethnically diverse—with almost 50 percent foreign-born people—than New York (36 percent) or Los Angeles (40 percent). Miami has a larger foreign-born population (59 percent), but that population is overwhelmingly Latino, while Toronto's immigrants come from the four corners.

7. John Ibbitson, "Can Only One Man See That Canada's Equalization Program Is Broken?" *Globe and Mail*, October 25, 2012.

Chapter 5

1. John Ibbitson, "How to Stop Demographic Suicide: Why Is Manitoba's Population Swelling, While Nova Scotia's Thins?" *Globe and Mail*, August 19, 2011.

2. Dave Cournoyer, "National Securities Regulator Shows Split Among Conservatives," *daveberta.ca—Alberta politics*, May 30, 2010, http://daveberta.ca/2010/05/national-securities-regulator-shows-split-among-conservatives/.

Chapter 6

1. Lawrence Martin, "Is This Still a Democracy? You Be the Judge," *iPolitics*, April 27, 2012, http://www.ipolitics.ca/2012/04/27/lawrence-martin-is-this-still-a-democracy-you-be-the-judge/.

2. Heather Mallick, "What If Harper's Dream of a Majority Comes True?" *Toronto Star*, March 28, 2011.

3. Stephen Clarkson, "Has the Centre Vanished?" *Literary Review of*

Canada, October 1, 2011, http://reviewcanada.ca
/essays/2011/10/01/has-the-centre-vanished/.

4. Erna Paris, "The New Solitudes," *The Walrus*, March 2011, http://
walrusmagazine.com/articles/2011.03-politics-the-new-solitudes/2/.

5. John Duffy, "Discipline of Powerlessness," *Policy Options*, March 2012.

6. Michael Den Tandt, "Mulcair's Clever but Cynical Tactic," *Ottawa Citizen*, May 14, 2012.

Chapter 7

1. Michael Den Tandt, "What a Difference a Year Doesn't Make," *Ottawa Citizen*, April 28, 2012.

2. John Ibbitson and André Pratte, "The Quebec Diaries," *Globe and Mail*, August 9, 2012.

Chapter 8

1. Frances Russell, "The Reality of Canada Is Fragile," *Winnipeg Free Press*, February 24, 2010.

2. Joe Friesen, "Why Canada Needs a Flood of Immigrants," *Globe and Mail*, May 4, 2012.

3. Patrick Grady and Herbert Grubel, *Immigration and the Canadian Welfare State 2011*, page v, Fraser Institute, http://fraserinstitute
.org/publicationdisplay.aspx?id=17546&terms=Immigration+and
+the+Canadian+Welfare+State+2011.

4. James Delinpole, "The Snow Must Go On in Vancouver," *Daily Telegraph*, February 10, 2010.

Chapter 10

1. Confidential sources.

Chapter 11

1. "Recorded Crime—Offenders, 2009–10," *Australian Bureau of Statistics*, http://www.abs.gov.au/ausstats/abs@.nsf/Products /5DC23AA21808ABB7CA257840000F31B9?opendocument.

2. Shelley Trevethan and Christopher J. Rastin, "A Profile of Visible Minority Offenders in the Federal Canadian Correctional System," *Correctional Service Canada*, http://www.csc-scc.gc.ca/text/rsrch /reports/r144/r144-eng.shtml#LinkTarget_24738.

3. Konrad Yakabusky, "Neither Practising Nor Believing, but Catholic Even So," *Globe and Mail*, August 15, 2009.

4. Kevin Dougherty, "National Assembly Turns Away Sikhs," Montreal *Gazette*, January 19, 2011.

5. Gilles Paquet, "About Dumbfounding Aspects of Canadian Immigration Policy," Centre on Governance, University of Ottawa, 2011, http://www.immigrationreform.ca/CMFiles/Research /Social%20cohesion/About%20%20the%20Dumbfounding%20 ... FINAL%20JUNE2011%20PDformat.pdf.

6. "About DC Public Charter Schools," *Friends of Choice in Urban Schools (FOCUS)*, http://focusdc.org/about-dc-public-charter-schools.

7. Andrew Vanacore, "Most New Orleans Charter Schools Outper-form Traditional Schools, Study Finds," *Times-Picayune*, March 18, 2011, http://www.nola.com/education/index.ssf/2011/03 /study_finds_most_new_orleans_c.html.

Chapter 12

1. D. Carment, F. Hampson, and N. Hillmer, eds., *Canada Among Nations 2004: Setting Priorities Straight*, Montreal and Kingston: McGill-Queen's University Press, 2005, page 84.

2. SIPRI Yearbook 2012, "World's Top 15 Military Spenders," cited in Wikipedia, http://en.wikipedia.org/wiki/List_of_countries_by_military_expenditures#SIPRI_Yearbook_2012_.E2.80.93_World.27s_top_15_military_spenders .

3. "GDP Growth (Annual %)," *The World Bank*, http://data.worldbank.org/indicator/NY.GDP.MKTP.KD.ZG.

4. Derek Burney and Fen Hampson, "How Obama Lost Canada: Botching Relations with the United States' Biggest Trade Partner," *Foreign Affairs*, June 21, 2012, http://www.foreignaffairs.com/articles/137744/derek-h-burney-and-fen-osler-hampson/how-obama-lost-canada.

5. Confidential sources.